Pearls of
Kitchen Wisdom

Also by Deborah S. Tukua

*Pearls of Country Wisdom:
Hints from a Small Town on Keeping
Garden and Home*

Pearls of Kitchen Wisdom

Tips, Shortcuts, and Recipes from a Country Home

By Deborah S. Tukua

THE LYONS PRESS

Designed by Compset, Inc.

Printed in the United States of America

10 9 8 7 6 5 4 3 2 1

All photographs by the author with the exception of page 86 by Ray Stafford

Library of Congress Cataloging-in-Publication Data

Tukua, Deborah, 1958–
    Pearls of kitchen wisdom: tips, shortcuts, and recipes from a country home/compiled and edited by Deborah S. Tukua.
        p. cm.
    Includes index.
    ISBN 1-58574-207-4
    1. Cookery. 2. Kitchens. I. Title.
    TX652.T85 2001
    641.5—dc21

                                                            00-67847

The tips and information in this book are intended to be a help to all who read them. They are not intended for use in place of professional medical advice. We cannot assume any liability or responsibility for any health, food preservation, or other advice given herein. Use at your discretion, please.

Contents

Dedication and Introduction

*Ointment and perfume rejoice in the heart: so doth the sweet-
ness of man's friend by hearty counsel.*

Proverbs 27:9

In life, each of us is strongly influenced by those close to
us. We are what we are because someone took the time to
invest in our lives. We learn by the example of others,
shared experiences, and personal instruction. I too have
benefited greatly from the wise counsel and influence of
others. To these people, more precious than pearls, I say
thanks for investing in me. Molded like clay on a potter's
wheel, so that I in turn am shaped and prepared to offer this
work herein to you this very moment in loving gratitude.

To:

Jesus Christ, my Savior and Lord, serving others in
love. While on this earth, Jesus cooked fish on the shores
of Galilee, refreshing his disciples, and setting forth the
example of hospitality and kindness. Ultimately, his

greatest act of love was paying the penalty of my sin so that I could be free to love because he first loved me.

My husband and best friend, Lowell Tukua, for winning me over with his culinary charms. He wooed me with a scrumptious Sunday dinner, although I tease and say that I married him for his mother's chocolate chip–oatmeal cookies. All kidding aside, many million thanks, as the Norwegians would say to you, dear husband, for being a man of vision, always looking ahead, encouraging me forward while living each day to the fullest, devoted in love! From you I have learned and continue to learn much.

My mother, Delores Stafford, at home in the kitchen, at home with family, friends, and everyone she greets with a warm smile, radiant eyes, and always a jovial laugh. She finds joy in pleasing others.

My friend Annette Godwin helped me get started in learning many country skills in the middle of suburbia. Annette taught me how to shop the farmer's market, make applesauce and apple jelly, and bake and preserve fresh pumpkin; she coached my first canning experience. Her husband, Hugh, taught me how to make whole-wheat bread by hand. It has been a pleasure to be introduced to such a gratifying and sufficient path and continue walking therein.

Once we moved from the city to the country in late June of 1995, learning opportunities multiplied rapidly. It was like learning a new language on the mission field. It's easier when you're among people who are speaking the language you want to learn. Thanks to: Deloris Massey, Ginger McNeil, Jeanne Mange, Arlene Nyhoff, Bonnie Plasse, Leslie Mullen, Darlene Millsapps, and the readers of *Coming Home* magazine for furthering my instruction and know-how in pressure-canning, cheese making, yogurt making, butter making, herbal teas, growing sprouts, juicing wheat grass, making homemade syrups and cereals. All rewarding, creative, and fun to learn.

And certainly to our children, David, Tiffany, and Josiah, for partaking willingly of Mama's experiments (new dishes) and often joining in the fun to help, reaping the benefits of wholesome country living.

There are so many different things to try within the framework of the kitchen. It's never boring at home, especially in the kitchen. The kitchen will truly be the heartbeat of your home when you set forth to learn and practice some of these valuable arts. And the best part of all is that you can start wherever you are right now, in whatever area of interest you choose. All that is essential is to have a friendly mentor to set you on your way. Learning how to make many of the things your family loves and needs is so gratifying. Making things yourself guarantees the quality of the product and your personal satisfaction. If you lack that encouraging friend to help you get started on the road to broadening your kitchen wisdom, I hope that you will turn to the helpful instruction within these pages. Pick a project, and let's get started. I love projects! And it's always more fun working with a good friend! I'll join you in the kitchen!

A cordial country greeting to you and yours,

Deborah S. Tukua

Acknowledgments

I wish to specifically express my gratitude to the following friends from whom I gathered pearls of wisdom for the kitchen in the form of a tip, hint, or help, assisting myself and henceforth others in becoming more skilled and efficient at the hearth of the home: Laine Amavizca, Debbie Bohannon, Mona Butler, Sadie Dibble, and Donna Prather.

Also, a hug and sincere thanks to Phyllis Stricklin, owner and operator of Main Street Treasures in Waynesboro, Tennessee, for allowing me to photograph her darling country-store displays and crafts for use in this book.

Thanks to Vicki West for allowing me to photograph her kitchen.

Hugs and kisses to Lowell, my love, for building my dream kitchen, where recipes are concocted and photographs were made.

To Becky Koh, editor, and the staff at Lyons Press for envisioning me in this project in the first place. Thank you for granting me creative liberty to present tips, helps, hints, and recipes, and to share within this book a little of myself from the heart and what I've gained from others.

To everyone who has shared recipes with me through the years. Some of our favorites are included.

Note

Although I do offer many practical pointers in preserving and canning foods as well as recipes, the step-by-step basics of canning are not included here. To the beginning canner, I suggest you acquire a copy of the latest Ball or County Extension Office Canning Guide for an equipment list and basic how-to-home-can information. Safe and successful canning to you!

Pearls of
Kitchen Wisdom

Country Kitchen Decor

The hearth of the home has always been the heart of activity and congregation. I suppose that's why so many people have returned to the spacious, open eat-in kitchen. To recapture the romance of farmsteads gone by, we've installed a wood-burning cookstove into our new country kitchen. It is prominently set up on a brick hearth as the focal point of the room. On the brick wall behind the stove hang cast-iron corn-bread pans, muffin tins, an antique copper dipper we found in the old barn on our homestead, and even one of Grannie's old pots. On the opposite side of the kitchen hangs a wide black pot rack that our son David hand-forged with his blacksmithing know-how. It handsomely displays a set of cast-iron cookware and echoes the rich blackness of the cookstove in our otherwise whitewashed kitchen. The huge 12" skillet and the other bulky griddles and pots are conveniently hung on this rack; this frees up cabinet space and keeps them within easy reach. Highly useful, usable items are attractive in their own right and therefore haven't been tucked away behind a closed closet or cabinet door. There is natural beauty in so many aspects of our daily life. It really isn't necessary to shop for things for the sole purpose of decorating our kitchen. Consider some charming common household items on hand already. A set of wood-handled cutlery can be attractively displayed while safely stored in a gallon glass jar. Gallon glass jars are handy for sorting and storing larger quantities of dried foodstuffs or cooking supplies and give a handsome general-store appeal painted by stencil in a country motif and lined up on an open kitchen cupboard. Produce baskets garnished with a gingham-checked ribbon are charmingly used to conceal bottles of vitamins, herbs, teas, cookie cutters, cake-decorating supplies, and more when lined up side by side on an open cupboard. Canning jars filled with bright red, orange, and green peppers, relishes, and produce in a rainbow assortment of colors give an open shelf unit the warmest sense of home.

At our kitchen window hangs a cute collection of blue-and-white handmade pot holders and a pair of blue-and-white rose-print oven mitts. Their convenient tab tops are strung neatly in a horizontal row on a wooden rod, serving as a charming and unique window valance. And the wide-plank pinewood floors would not be complete in this homey kitchen without several cushy fabric rugs to sink your bare toes into while washing dishes or stirring a savory stew on the wood cookstove.

☙ 1 ❧

The kitchen is the hearth and heart of the home.

☙ 2 ❧

Common household items can add charm to your kitchen when properly displayed. Save gallon glass jars for storage. A set of cutlery knives with wooden handles can be safely and handsomely housed in a glass jar.

Fill other jars with cookie cutters, dried fruits, pop-corn, sugar, beans, etc., and store on an open shelf. To lend a further country flair, paint apples, sunflowers, bears, or hearts using stencils on the front of each jar. Not all shelves or cabinets in a country kitchen need doors.

3

Who says canisters have to match? Select old or interesting canisters that complement the decor to attractively store your dry goods.

4

An old wire basket can be hung on the wall to attractively house rolling pins when not in use. A collection of rolling pins can also be handsomely stored in an expandable wine rack.

₭ 5 ₭

Tin cans serve as inexpensive and cute country flower pots or vases. Save large steel vegetable cans with imprinted logo and vegetable graphics. Put strips of masking tape across the opening in a crisscross fashion. This will help hold upright fresh-picked flowers. Also, save any metal olive oil containers. Remove the top with a can opener and use as a container for fresh-cut flowers, a potted plant, or a silk floral arrangement.

₭ 6 ₭

Here's a cute and unique window-treatment idea: Hang a charming collection of hot pads, pot holders, or oven mitts by the tabs on a dowel rod over the kitchen window as a valance.

❦ 7 ❦

An old broomstick makes a good curtain rod, especially with café rings or tab-type curtains.

❦ 8 ❦

Sandwich ferns, foliage, and flat flowers between two clear-glass plates to spruce up each place setting at your next luncheon. Plates can be made up the day before and kept in the refrigerator. Remove from the refrigerator 30 minutes before serving.

❦ 9 ❦

The easiest of all ways to hang kitchen curtains is to string up a clothesline at the kitchen window and peg or clothespin curtains or kitchen towels to the line.

🦋 *10* 🦋

Ever hear of stringing leather britches? It's what the pioneers called their technique for drying green beans. Try this the next time you grow green beans in your garden. Using a needle and thin string or heavy thread, thread green beans, one after another. Repeat the process until you have enough strings of green beans to hang vertically at your kitchen window. A window valance straight from the garden!

🦋 *11* 🦋

Burlap makes great rustic window curtains for your kitchen and comes in a variety of colors. Look for old cotton tote sacks, which were used in the field, at antiques stores or flea markets.

❧ *12* ❧

Make a window valance for the kitchen or dining-room window using large cloth dinner napkins, place mats, or bandannas. Arrange on an inside mounting board, overlapping slightly with the points down, and staple. Affix to the top of the window with a drill and screws.

❧ *13* ❧

Cute country curtains can be made from kitchen towels. Coordinate with your existing towels and colors. Sew two kitchen towels together lengthwise. Then sew matching trim or tiebacks at the seam for either side of the window. Or select a variety of coordinating kitchen towels (enough to cover the window's width); sew a rod pocket, grosgrain ribbon, or tabs at the top of each and insert or tie onto a curtain rod.

✺ 14 ✺

Cute country curtain tiebacks can be easily assembled by stringing old wooden thread spools onto twine. To add more color, wrap colored yarn onto each spool and glue the ends to secure.

❦ *15* ❦

When you go rustic, you'll never need to buy curtain rods again. Choose a branch or sapling that has a fork in it. You'll need two of these to support the rod. Cut both branches about 3" beneath the fork. With a drill, screw both rod supports to the wall in two places about 1" apart. Select a fairly straight complementary "rod" from the same tree species. Saw to the length needed. Window curtains with tab tops lend themselves well to this type of rod.

❦ *16* ❦

Cut out desired images, shapes, or designs from wallpaper: for example, farm animals, flowers, garden vegetables, etc. Place them in a horizontal row on the wall to form a unique wallpaper border. Or use to adorn benches or baskets.

❦ 17 ❦

Benches yield the most seating. Also, if you buy or make them with boxes beneath and a flip-top seat/lid, you've got an extra space for storage of tablecloths, place mats, the leaf for a table, or other long items.

❦ 18 ❦

Next time you purchase or build an island in the kitchen, consider one with wheels and hinged drop-leaf pieces on two sides. Pull up stools and you've got a great place to serve a simple dinner for two. Roll the island into the dining room on such occasions when you need to accommodate overflow from the dining table.

❦ *19* ❦

Here's a conversation piece for displaying pots, pans, and cooking utensils. Acquire an old wagon wheel and suspend it from the ceiling by four chains. Put S hooks on the spokes of the wheel to hang your cookware.

❦ *20* ❦

Cups taking up too much room in the cupboard? Place cup hooks beneath a cabinet or on a thin strip of wood mounted on the wall horizontally. You'll free up cabinet space while attractively and efficiently displaying your cups.

❦ *21* ❦

Old quilts make lovely table coverings indoors or out.

🦋 22 🦋

Have an old quilt too worn to use for a tablecloth? Cut out squares that are in good condition to make place mats, seat cushions, or even throw pillows for a bench in the kitchen.

🦋 23 🦋

Here's a treasure. If you ever run across one, grab it. An old double-deck, metal chicken laying unit with multiple round openings makes an absolutely adorable storage system for your kitchen. The wooden strip along the bottom can hold S hooks or cup hooks to hang coffee cups or equipment. The bins could display plates or canning goods antique country style.

🪱 24 🪱

Straight-back chair need a new seat? Try tightly inter-weaving men's neckties for a colorful seat. Use a staple gun to affix the basket-weave ties to the underside of the chair frame. The same effect can be accomplished with men's wide suspenders, too!

🪱 25 🪱

Refrigerator/Photo Album

Wondering what to do with all those photographs received during the holidays? Arrange them attractively on a sheet of construction paper and glue into place. Note the date, and place them on the refrigerator with magnets. At the end of the year, when new photographs start coming in, remove the old sheet and start a new one. When retiring a year of photographs, punch holes along one side of the sheet and start an album. Make a front and back cover from poster board. Join together with yarn, twine, or ribbon and you've got an organized collection of photographs.

🦋 26 🦋

Here's a handy, clever, and very attractive way to keep important numbers by the telephone in the kitchen. Purchase a small louver shutter, 7" wide × 20" long. Place a blank sticky label on each side of the center piece of the louvers when in the open position and fill in with important names and telephone numbers. When finished, close the louvers and the numbers will be tucked away until needed again. With stencils, sponge-paint a decoration on the front of the shutter to match the interior of the room and hang on the wall nearest the telephone.

🦋 27 🦋

Expensive cabinet doors not in the budget for a new cabinet, or prefer something a little different? Consider using shutters instead. Attach them to the cabinet with hinges, and drill holes for the hardware.

🕭 *28* 🕭

Bring the fragrant scents of spring and summer indoors. Place a trellis right outside your kitchen or breakfast-room window. Grow jasmine, wisteria, honeysuckle, or other strongly fragrant vines. Or plant a gardenia bush. Pray for a nice breeze and don't forget to leave the windows open.

🕭 *29* 🕭

Coordinate the dining table and window coverings. Purchase two tablecloths—one sized to fit the table; the other one, rectangular, to twist and drape from a decorative rod. Trim the excess to fit the window lengthwise, and hem. Save the excess to make napkins.

❦ *30* ❦

Everyone appreciates a candlelight dinner. Bring country charm to your dinner table. Fill several canning jars one-quarter full of sand (or salt). Add a votive candle to each jar and tie a gingham bow around the outside of the jar.

❦ *31* ❦

Here's another table centerpiece using glassware. Have any old-fashioned parfait glasses on hand? Turn them upside down and top with votive candles. Place some right-side up, fill with marbles, and add a tea light or votive candle. Add a glass banana boat to the center of the table filled with votive candles and you'll bring back memories of the good old days at the soda-fountain shop.

❧ *32* ❧

A snazzy way to dress up straight-back chairs in the kitchen is to place a colorful vest on each.

🐦 *33* 🐦

Circles of wooden slabs sawn off a log (from the local sawmill) make sturdy, durable pot and casserole trivets for the porch, picnic, or rustic kitchen table. Dip in tung oil or polyurethane.

🐦 *34* 🐦

Mount legs on a thick circular slab of wood to construct a chopping block.

🐦 *35* 🐦

A natural onion braid is a welcome friend in the country kitchen. Fresh onions from the garden work best, as the tops need to be flexible enough to braid. Select three large, attractive onions with long stems and braid together. Secure the braided stems in place by tying with twine or raffia. Start adding in more onions, alternating sides and in the middle, every inch or so, working the tops into the existing braid. Continue securing with twine as you go. When the onion braid has reached an attractive length, finish braiding the ends and loop around and secure with twine to form a loop hanger at the top. Onions store best in a cool, dry place. Best not to hang onion braids by the stove.

36

Give your kitchen that country-store charm. Line enough baskets in a row to fill an open shelf. Attractively store herbs, vitamins, picnic supplies, cookie cutters, and other miscellaneous items. Spruce up the baskets with a trim of checked or gingham ribbon around the top. Ask your neighborhood grocer about buying his used produce baskets instead of purchasing them from a large craft store. I bought three baskets for the price of one this way.

🦋 *37* 🦋

Perk up an open shelf unit by making fabric bags in co-ordinating patterns and colors of ticking and gingham or from kitchen towels and use for storing bags of flour, dry mixes, rice, dried beans, dried fruit, and the like. (Bags can be washed and reused.)

🦋 *38* 🦋

Home-canned jars of fruits and vegetables are especially attractive on your kitchen shelf when topped with a circle of fabric and tied with a ribbon.

❦ 39 ❦

Make your own hanging lamp shade from a large color-ful ceramic bowl turned upside down. Drill a hole in the center to fit with electrical kit, lightbulb, and chain, and suspend over a kitchen sink or table. The wash-basin from an old washstand works well for this project.

❦ 40 ❦

Metal cookie cutters double nicely as napkin rings on the kitchen table. (Spray-paint to match the decor, if desired.)

🎴 *41* 🎴

Place a handsome washstand and basin in your dining room and put it to use on festive occasions. Add water, floating candles, and flowers to the washbasin for a romantic country dinner.

🎴 *42* 🎴

When there're appetizers or cake and punch to be served, try this original idea with a country flair. You'll need a charming washstand with ceramic basin and pitcher. Fill the washbasin with punch. Ladle into ½-pint canning jars for individual serving cups. Use the pitcher to refill the washbasin for a quaint party setting. Try this idea at your next country wedding reception.

🦋 43 🦋

An old-fashioned washbasin makes a good fruit bowl display. If you have a stand with a basin and pitcher to go along, load it all up with fresh fruit and nuts. It creates a lovely visual welcome when you're receiving overnight guests.

🦋 44 🦋

Need a kitchen or dining-room wall decoration? Display your plates! Yes, the ones you use to serve at mealtime. No need to keep your lovely plates hidden when not in use. Hang them on an iron rack or wooden plate shelf. And if you use them regularly, there will be no need to dust. Less expensive than a painting, highly functional and convenient.

🦋 45 🦋

For efficient living, eliminate figurines from your decorating. Replace with usable items such as an antique serving tray, baskets, cookie jars, canisters, rolling pins, etc. For less clutter and less time spent cleaning, the items in your home should be as functional and practical as they are attractive.

🦋 46 🦋

Adopt this philosophy: "The house and its furnishings should serve you instead of you serving the house."

❦ *47* ❦

Need more storage-shelf space in the kitchen? Take advantage of often wasted space over the kitchen window, doorways, and around the upper portion of walls. Install shelves for glassware, cookbooks, baskets, or other handsome items.

🐜 *48* 🐜

Apron Holder

On a narrow strip of oak or pine, drill holes spaced several inches apart and affix either vintage glass doorknobs or ceramic or glass cabinet knobs. (Select the same or coordinating hardware with cabinetry.) Mount the finished piece on the wall horizontally to attractively display lovely kitchen aprons.

Organization, Efficiency, Cleanup, and Safety

The nuts and bolts of an efficiently functioning kitchen lie in its organization. There is no character quality I admire more in a woman than the gift of organization. I suppose it's because moms have so many people, places, and things to keep up with on any given day. Recently, our family visited a girls' home and academy in rural Mississippi. I was amazed. In that tiny galley-style kitchen, food was prepared by the gallon for a dozen hungry, growing girls. This remarkable home was run by one loving couple. They did it all within a very limited space: schooling, crafting, counseling, and more. The lady of the house was also the cook. When she makes biscuits, she makes a hundred at a time. She served up a gallon of mashed potatoes, roast turkey, a quart or two of turkey gravy, biscuits, vegetables, and iced tea, and she wasn't even out of breath afterward. In fact, she had it so together that she invited me into the kitchen to visit with her while she put the finishing touches on everything.

I watched as they all went about their business, industrious as ants. Everyone had a job to do. As one girl set the table, the house mother watched through the window opening from the kitchen into the dining hall and corrected her when she hurriedly dropped silverware on the table. "If she doesn't learn how to set a table at this age, she won't know how to do it right when she gets married either," the house mother said. Another girl placed all the condiments out for the buffet spread while yet another filled the glasses with ice and tea. While we chatted in the kitchen, another girl was washing up the bowls from preparing the meal. She asked the house mother how to remove something from the rim of a plastic container. Her substitute mom gave her the answer without missing a stir of the gravy pot. I could see these dozen girls walking about, performing household duties, smiling, and being cordial. They were patterning after this lady whom I would definitely put in the ranks of the virtuous woman spoken of so highly in Proverbs 31. When it was time for our family to say good-bye, the girls gathered together and sang two songs a cappella just for us. They sang willingly and boldly from the heart. All virtuous women in the making, I'd say.

I couldn't help but feel a little guilty. We'd just moved into a brand-new house that we built on our property, and my *kitchen is so much roomier. We too have taken in children through adoption to love and help. But we have lots of room to spare in comparison. Our numbers are few. This lady is using every inch of space she has to the best of her ability, providing a lifeline and future hope for the next generation and, best of all, to the glory of God.*

🦋 *49* 🦋

If things are put in their proper place, you should be able to find them blindfolded!

🦋 *50* 🦋

"A place for everything and everything in its place."

🦋 *51* 🦋

Make fewer trips back and forth from the car on grocery day by carrying groceries in a cardboard box. Leave a box with hand grips in the car trunk for grocery day.

🦋 *52* 🦋

In the hot summer, an ice chest is a handy and practical item to have along, especially if you must drive thirty miles or more into town. An ice chest keeps orange juice and ice cream fresh on the drive home.

🦋 *53* 🦋

Cleaning up the kitchen doesn't consist of merely clearing the table and washing the dishes. Here's a checklist for you to use in training your children to be efficient and thorough when on kitchen duty. (Copy and post for daily checkoff.)

✔ Table cleared and wiped clean?

✔ All dishes, pots, and cooking equipment washed and put away?

✔ Kitchen sink clean and faucet wiped dry?

✔ Countertops and stove wiped clean and free of clutter?

✔ Dish towels and dishcloths hung up properly to dry?

✔ Floor swept well, especially under the table?

✔ Chairs pushed back under the table neatly?
✔ Kitchen looks as clean and orderly as you'd want it to if guests were coming?

🦋 *54* 🦋

Keep your kitchen broom from wearing out sooner than necessary. Always store the broom off the floor, hung by a hook or peg on the wall or the back of a door.

🦋 *55* 🦋

Avoid "dishpan" hands. Add a teaspoon of baking soda to the dish-washing water.

🦋 56 🦋

Pot, pan, or Corningware burned? Put baking soda in
the bottom of the pan and let it sit awhile before washing. The char should come out easily.

🦋 57 🦋

Help cut grease when washing pots and pans. Pour a
capful of ammonia into the soapy dishwater (but see
tip #58).

🦋 58 🦋

Never add ammonia to dishwater when washing aluminum cookware.

🦋 *59* 🦋

Clean your kitchen easily. Fill a clean trigger spray bottle with warm water and 6 to 8 tablespoons of ammonia. Use to clean the stove top, counters, sink, and small appliances.

🦋 *60* 🦋

Remove greasy fingerprints and scuff marks with full-strength ammonia.

🦋 *61* 🦋

For a mild cleanser, try an application of borax on porcelain and aluminum cookware. Sprinkle borax on pots and pans as you would any powdered cleanser and rub with a damp dishcloth. Borax won't scratch.

❦ 62 ❦

Wash glassware in an automatic dishwasher? Reduce water spotting by adding a tablespoon of powdered borax to each load. Or add a little to your dishpan when washing glassware by hand.

❦ 63 ❦

Especially when baking, keep warm sudsy water in the kitchen sink. As soon as you remove a loaf of bread from its pan, muffins from a tin, or a cake from a cake pan, place in the sink to soak. It makes later cleaning of these baking items so much easier.

❧ *64* ❧

Make cleaning the inside of the microwave easier by first heating a cup of water until it boils. The moisture inside will help loosen the food particles, etc.

❧ *65* ❧

Position the refrigerator several inches from the wall to the rear; never locate next to the kitchen range or other heat-generating appliances.

❧ *66* ❧

Finally, a way to stop those ugly pit marks from forming on your refrigerator door! Coat the outer surface of the refrigerator with car wax once a year. (Unless it's stainless steel, of course.)

✯ 67 ✯

Here's a way to determine if your refrigerator or freezer is holding in the cool air sufficiently. Close the refrigerator door on a slip of notebook paper. If the paper pulls out easily, you are losing energy and efficiency. Time to replace the seal around the door.

✯ 68 ✯

Going out of town for a few days? Save energy consumption by turning the cold control of the refrigerator down to a lower setting until you return. (If you don't, you may return to find ice crystals on your fresh produce, etc.)

🦋 69 🦋

Never place hot dishes or foods in the refrigerator. Cover and allow to cool to the touch first. And never place dishes cold from the refrigerator directly into a hot oven.

🦋 70 🦋

Here is absolutely the easiest way to clean the top of your refrigerator. Drape a towel or table scarf across the top. It's so much easier to remove the cloth and wash it than it is to climb on a chair and scrub the fridge top.

🦋 71 🦋

To clean the blender with little effort, squirt in some dish soap and fill three-quarters full of water. Blend for 2 minutes. Wipe out with a dishcloth and rinse.

72

Need help opening a jar? Wear latex gloves for a better grip.

73

Save plastic bags and ties from store-bought goods to store homemade bread, muffins, etc.

74

Reseal opened pretzel, chip, yeast, cornmeal, flour, and sugar bags with a clothespin or a clamp-style trouser hanger.

❧ 75 ❧

A plastic gallon ice-cream bucket with a lid is handy for storing food scraps after every meal. When full, feed to the chickens or compost pile.

❧ 76 ❧

Remove rust stains from stainless-steel sinks by applying baking soda and allowing to sit overnight. Rub into the area and rinse the next morning.

❧ 77 ❧

Remove water spots from a stainless-steel sink or faucet with an application of rubbing alcohol or vinegar.

🐜 *78* 🐜

Dishes stacked in the cupboard? Prevent scratches by placing a paper doily between plates and saucers.

🐜 *79* 🐜

Gone are the days of polishing silver! Here's a much better way to remove tarnish from silver flatware. Place an aluminum cake or pie pan in the bottom of a large enamel kettle. Measure water into the kettle. Add 1 tablespoon each of baking soda and salt for each quart of water used. Bring to a boil. Put the silver flatware to be cleaned into the kettle. Ensure that each piece either touches the aluminum pan or another piece of silver flatware that is touching the pan. Boil 2 to 5 minutes. Remove the silver, wash, and dry. Buff to a soft polish with a flannel cloth.

🐉 *80* 🐉

Need to deodorize jars and bottles that you wish to save and reuse? Pour a solution of water and dry mustard in each container and let stand for a few hours before the final wash and rinse.

🐉 *81* 🐉

Problems with sugar ants in the pantry and on kitchen countertops? Place some peppermint oil or clove oil on a cloth and wipe the shelves and countertops where ants are a nuisance.

🐉 *82* 🐉

Toss a bay leaf into each kitchen canister to keep pests out of pasta, flour, rice, and dry mixes.

🦋 *83* 🦋

A bowl of assorted fresh fruits is a lovely table dressing. Sprinkle some bay leaves among the fruits to deter fruit flies.

🦋 *84* 🦋

Make cleanup time easy by spraying the grater with a light coat of cooking oil before using it to grate chocolate, cheeses, or vegetables.

🦋 *85* 🦋

Oil your measuring cups or spoons before measuring molasses, honey, or peanut butter. The contents will slide out easily, leaving no waste.

❦ 86 ❧

Measuring out shortening can be quite messy. Use an ice-cream scoop. A standard-size scoop holds ¼ cup. Scoop out the shortening and plop into place. No greasy measuring cup and spatula to clean afterward.

❦ 87 ❧

A toothbrush is a handy tool in the kitchen for cleaning utensils such as potato peelers, food graters, beaters, can-opener blades, etc.

❦ 88 ❧

Forgot a boiling pot on the stove and now it's a burnt mess? No need to throw the pot away. Cover the bottom of the pot with baking soda and water. Bring to a boil and maintain the boil for 5 to 10 minutes. Allow to cool, then pour off the water and the charred residue. Repeat the process a second time, if needed.

❦ *89* ❦

Eliminate messy cleanup after making bread. Mix bread ingredients and knead the dough in the same large, wide bowl. No floured surface to clean afterward!

❦ *90* ❦

Remove strong fish odor from cooking utensils and pans by adding a few tablespoons of ammonia to the dishwater (but see tip #58).

⚜ *91* ⚜

No time to wash your hands when a child falls or the phone rings? Keep a pair of deep plastic storage bags handy for such times. Just slip on like a glove and clean up later when time allows.

⚜ *92* ⚜

When preparing jelly or other messy-type sandwiches for young children, serve in a plastic sandwich bag. Slide the sandwich up as needed, allowing all the drips to be caught in the bag! Great for preserving clothes during picnics or when serving a host of children.

⚜ *93* ⚜

Before you use a new cast-iron skillet, it must be seasoned. To do so, first wash with a mild dish-washing liquid, rinse, and dry. Then coat the pan with lard or vegetable shortening and bake in the oven for one and a half hours at 300°F. (Or follow manufacturer's instructions.) Season again whenever the cookware shows sign of rust.

🐜 94 🐜

Use a plastic scouring pad instead of metal when scrubbing cast-iron cookware.

🐜 95 🐜

If you must store your cast-iron skillets stacked on top of one another, line with a paper plate, napkin, or disposable coffee filter.

🦋 96 🦋

To keep your iron skillets from rusting, apply a thin coating of shortening or vegetable oil to the inside surface after washing. Never stack skillets damp. After washing, set them on a warm stove top for quick drying. Then oil them and put away.

🦋 97 🦋

Rust on your cast-iron cookware? Rub with salt and re-season. See tip #93.

🦋 98 🦋

A square skillet holds more than a round one.

99

Time to refill the saltshaker? Cover the bottom of your saltshaker with raw rice. Then add the salt as usual. This will keep the salt from absorbing moisture and allow it to flow easily.

100

Keep your kitchen scissors sharp by cutting a piece of sandpaper with them periodically.

101

Wonder why the old-timers never contracted *Salmonella?* After using a cutting board, they thoroughly cleaned and heavily salted it.

❧ *102* ❧

Here's how a retired meat cutter from Minnesota protected cutting boards from bacteria. First, clean the board well. Then apply a little bleach-water solution and rinse. Dry completely. Melt paraffin in an old double boiler. Pour enough paraffin over the board to cover it thoroughly. Take a hot iron (worn electric or sad iron warmed on a wood or coal cookstove) and iron the wax into the board. The melted wax and the ironing process seal any cracks or open pores in the wood. (This procedure should be repeated periodically as the wax wears away.)

❧ *103* ❧

Use washable wallpaper to efficiently line pantry and cabinet shelves.

❧ *104* ❧

Organize your kitchen cabinets by the job. Locate all storage containers together. Designate one cabinet as the baking center and furnish with baking trays, cookie sheets, rolling pins, etc. Another cabinet for canning will be furnished with canner, jar lifter, pectin, funnels, canning-jar lids and rings, etc. If you have a special hobby such as cheese making or cake decorating, a shelf or two should be allotted for easy retrieval of necessary tools. When everything needed for a particular task is located together, you'll be less apt to put the job off.

❧ *105* ❧

Save steps in the kitchen by positioning foods and utensils at "points of first use." Canned foods should be close to the can opener. Mixing bowls, sugar, flour, and seasonings should be near the mixing center. Pots and pans should be near the stove. The grater, blender, or food processor should be placed on a counter close to the refrigerator. Potatoes, carrots, and other vegetables needing to be scrubbed should be stored close to the sink. A properly organized kitchen complements the cook and assists in saving time and energy.

🦋 *106* 🦋

Keep little things from getting lost in the drawers. Use an egg carton to sort and house cake-decorating tips and other tiny but important items in the kitchen drawers.

🦋 *107* 🦋

We've all been instructed on the values of making a grocery list. Always keep a pad of paper and pen on the refrigerator as a running list. The more often you go to the store, the more you spend! Take your list so you won't forget something and have to run back. Who ever buys just one thing when she goes into the supermarket?

❦ *108* ❦

Save coupons? As soon as you clip a new coupon, put it directly in your wallet with your bills. This way you will see it at checkout time, when it's needed.

❦ *109* ❦

Little one learning how to feed himself? Place the top from a plastic, gallon ice-cream bucket upside down under your toddler's bowl to catch any milk or other foods that might spill.

❦ *110* ❦

Serving children a picnic meal outdoors? Save the individual cups and lids from yogurt to serve drinks or ice cream outdoors. No spills or broken glass when the cups are carried outside with the lids on. These cups are sturdy and don't crack easily. Discard, or wash and reuse on your next outing.

🦋 *111* 🦋

Taking stuffed eggs to a picnic? A clean egg carton is perfect for protecting the eggs during the trip.

🦋 *112* 🦋

Don't confuse your serving pieces of flatware when taking them to a family reunion or group dinner. Paint your last initial or a symbol on the handle back with fingernail polish.

❧ *113* ❧

Keep brown sugar soft by refrigerating it in a glass jar or plastic bag with a piece of bread or apple.

❧ *114* ❧

Want to melt baker's chocolate without a messy pot to clean afterward? Here's how. Wrap chocolate squares in additional foil and melt in a double boiler. Once it's melted, carefully spoon out the chocolate.

❧ *115* ❧

Do you make cookies, bread, pancakes, or biscuits often? Instead of pulling out the ingredients daily and mixing just one batch at a time, mix several batches at one time, minus the liquid ingredients. Put one batch of ingredients into a separate Ziploc bag or other air-tight container. Label the contents and store in the refrigerator or freezer. On each bag write the quantities of wet ingredients to be added during final preparation time. These make great gift or bazaar sale items when placed in a lovely fabric bag with bow and recipe card. (See Pumpkin-Banana Pancakes, tip #407, for an example of making mixes.)

☙ 116 ❧

Make every step count twice when cooking. When browning fresh ground meat, fry enough for at least two meals. Use the portion required for that meal and refrigerate extra to use within the week, or freeze. Follow the same suggestion when boiling chicken or baking a ham. Prepare more than just one meal's quantity at a time. Make two meat loaves and freeze one. Or shape meatballs and bake them in the oven. Can or freeze in meal portions for future convenience.

🐝 *117* 🐝

Save time and nutritional value. Leave the peels on your potatoes, even when making casseroles, potato salad, and mashed potatoes!

🐝 *118* 🐝

Save cooking time and fuel consumption by grating potatoes, onions, and carrots when making soup.

🐝 *119* 🐝

When preparing meat loaf, put it in lightly oiled muffin tins to reduce cooking time and to avoid heating up the kitchen. No loaf to slice; it's all ready to serve in individual portions.

❦ *120* ❦

When using a double boiler, add a few marbles to the bottom pot with the water. If the water boils out of the bottom pot, the marbles will sound the alarm.

❦ *121* ❦

Need to put out a fire on the stovetop? Douse the fire with salt.

❦ *122* ❦

A siphon bottle of seltzer makes a handy fire extinguisher when kept near the stove (but do *not* use this on a grease fire).

❧ *123* ❧

Keep a potted aloe plant on your kitchen windowsill to treat minor burns. When needed, break off a stem, slice open the flesh, and rub the gel from the inside of the aloe plant directly on the burn.

❧ *124* ❧

Never leave anything flammable, such as a towel, pot holder, etc., on the top of any stove.

❧ *125* ❧

Always melt butter over low heat to avoid a fire.

Baking
and Cake
Decorating

There's something soothing and secure about a warm loaf of bread fresh out of a hot oven. Fond are the recollections of my grandmother rolling out buttermilk biscuits on her well-floured kitchen table top. She cut each one uniformly with the top of a drinking glass. During my visit she'd serve me one with a pat of butter and cream cheese. That was when I had a toothpick frame and didn't have to concern myself with fat intake or counting calories.

Every Thanksgiving, we looked forward to Grannie's homemade pumpkin pies and pecan pies and baked turkey with corn-bread dressing. My grandparents' house was modest in size, but nobody seemed to notice. We pulled up every bench, stool, and chair we could find to seat us all. The Jacobs family's dinners were special because Grannie made them special. It wasn't because the meals were served in a palace or a showplace. Grannie Jacobs served up her banquet dinners from the heart, making everything from scratch.

When Grannie passed away, I felt it my duty and an honor to carry on her tradition. I made sure not to let one family holiday dinner pass without making the traditional pastry shells and homemade pies from scratch. I knew I could never measure up to Grannie in setting forth such a spread, but to make her pumpkin pie and pecan pie recipes at each holiday dinner was to keep her memory alive in our hearts and to carry the tradition into the next generation. My mother, who has lovingly earned the title as the reigning Grannie, makes turkey and gravy and corn-bread dressing just like her mom. And even though my maternal grandmother didn't live long enough to know my children, in essence they have known the serving, loving, giving, jovial part of her through my mother, their grannie.

Fresh-baked goods are a gift from home and the heart. The kitchen is the heartbeat of the home. What warms the heart more when away, whether at college or in the armed forces, than when a letter and package arrive with Mama's cookies? When that box arrives, roommates gather around to beg a taste of home, too. Even if it's not their own. When Lowell and I were first getting acquainted, he shared a gallon bucket of chocolate chip–oatmeal cookies with me that his mother baked and mailed to him from Hartland, Minnesota. I still kid him and say that I married him for his mother's cookies! Nowadays, Grandma Tukua sends cookies to our children on birthdays and other special occasions. It warms the heart to know that someone cares enough to bake something special for us. To take the time to create something for others is truly an expression of love.

Cinnamon rolls or cinnamon-raisin bread is the perfect way to start the morning. A loaf of whole-wheat bread with tasty bits of dried tomato, oregano, and basil at noon; delicious brown bread baked with molasses in the evening. When it's topped with honey-butter and cinnamon spread, that's living. Who wouldn't stay close to home at mealtime? And who doesn't like to be around when Mama's baking a cake? It's pure luxury to lick the beaters and run your index finger around the mixing bowl to get that last scoop of icing. The benefits of the family that bakes together. Nothing perks up the kitchen more than the fragrance of fresh pies, pastries, cakes, and bread in the oven. The fragrance of home sentimentally etched in the senses.

One family we dearly love bakes brownies and homemade pizza together every Friday night. Then they play games together as a family. Their children delight in staying home, teens included! That's right. They prefer to spend their Friday nights at home with the family. Certainly, there is much more involved here than merely baked goods. They are tying heartstrings, being knitted together in love. Memories in the making! When we consistently and affectionately pour love and a cheerful spirit before our family, we're offering our best from the heart. Nothing the world has to offer can top that, even on a Friday night.

🐝 *126* 🐝

Need cake flour? Spoon 2 T. of cornstarch into a measuring cup. Fill the cup with all-purpose flour to the 1 c. mark. Sift together three times and use in any recipe calling for 1 c. cake flour.

🐝 *127* 🐝

Place flour in a saltshaker and shake when needed, or use a powder puff to neatly dust bread boards and other pastry-working surfaces with flour.

🐝 *128* 🐝

When making sponge cake, especially angel food, remove eggs from the refrigerator several hours before using. They beat up lighter and make finer cake when they're not cold.

❦ *129* ❦

Eggs should be room temperature before mixing in batters when baking. Set chilled eggs out 30 minutes before starting.

❦ *130* ❦

Biscuit dough makes the tastiest pie shell and top crust when preparing chicken potpie.

❦ *131* ❦

Vitamin C helps sustain the leavening of bread during baking. It also promotes yeast growth, causing your yeast to work longer and faster, and helps promote the acidic atmosphere in which yeast grows best. To liquids, add ¼ t. vitamin C powder or a 250 mg. tablet, crushed, per four-loaf bread recipe.

132

"Enriched bread" from the grocery-store shelves usually contains only four of the thirty vitamins found in fresh whole-wheat flour! In 72 hours, 90 percent of the thirty nutrients oxidize. Bake with fresh-ground flour and store excess in the freezer to retain the nutrients.

133

The liquid reserved after boiling potatoes gives greater volume yet a coarser texture to bread, one that is good for holding spread butter after toasting. Potato water also adds moistness. Use for no more than half of the liquid requirements in any bread recipe.

🐦 *134* 🐦

Want to cut down on fat when baking? Substitute applesauce for cooking oil in any cake recipe.

🐦 *135* 🐦

For a really pretty presentation, bake your next pumpkin-bread or banana-bread recipe in small, greased coffee cans. It slices into attractive round cakes.

🐦 *136* 🐦

When baking chocolate cakes, dust greased cake pans with cocoa or carob powder instead of flour.

❧ *137* ❧

Carob powder may be used as a noncaffeine, healthy substitute for cocoa powder.

❧ *138* ❧

Decorate a frosted cake or cheesecake with designs from quilting or craft templates. Lay the desired template on the cake top. Then sprinkle on powdered sugar or colored sugar crystals. Remove the template and voilà.

🎋 *139* 🎋

Want to decorate a cake, but not feeling artistic? Select a cookie cutter in the design of your choice and press into the icing. Pipe around the shape with icing in a second color and fill in as desired.

❦ *140* ❦

An inexpensive product to use in place of sprinkles when decorating cakes is flavored, colored gelatin powder!

❦ *141* ❦

Flowers are lovely, even on cakes. And some are edible. Garnish your next festive cake with some freshly picked edible varieties of rosebuds or rose petals, violets, pansies, or clover.

❦ *142* ❦

It's easy to tint coconut flakes for decorating cakes and other desserts. Place shredded coconut in a glass jar, not more than half full. Squirt in a few drops of liquid coloring. Cover the jar and shake until the color has blended throughout.

❧ *143* ❧

Need a cooling rack large enough to cool a sheet cake? Remove a rack from your oven before heating.

❧ *144* ❧

To keep your cake-cooling rack from making imprints on cakes, first lay a piece of net fabric across the top of the rack.

❧ *145* ❧

Cake too dry? Moisten it before serving. Randomly poke holes at least three-quarters through the cake vertically using thin wooden skewers. Pour a fruit syrup across the top and allow it to soak through before serving. (See the fruit syrup recipes, tips #404, 406, and 422, in the recipe section.)

✺ *146* ✺

It's difficult to spread cold icing on a cake. To warm, set the bowl of icing into a larger bowl containing hot water, and use a warm knife to spread the icing.

✺ *147* ✺

Here's a great way to protect cakes while transporting to a dinner, home, etc. Place sheet cakes in a cardboard box with sides and slide all within a plastic bag. Leave air in the bag. If something or someone taps the top of the cake by accident, the air in the bag will prevent the cake from receiving the blow.

❦ 148 ❦

To successfully cut a square or rectangular cake, slice a quarter section at a time. This should keep it from collapsing.

❦ 149 ❦

To easily slice cheesecakes and frosted cakes, dip the knife in hot water. Dry off to prevent the frosting and cake crumbs from sticking to it.

🎋 *150* 🎋

Gingerbread cookies are too tasty to enjoy only once a year. Embellish them with shawls, aprons, hats, or bonnets, and they become Pilgrims at Thanksgiving.

❦ *151* ❦

Don't make cheese and fresh bread the same day, as one will not turn out properly.

❦ *152* ❦

When you're making pie dough, recipes often instruct you to cut the butter into the flour with two butter knives. Here's an easier way. Using chilled, firm butter, grate by hand into the bowl.

❦ *153* ❦

To keep pie shells from forming bubbles, lay a stainless-steel pull chain (ceiling-fan size) in a coil in the bottom of your unbaked pie shell and bake as usual.

⚶ *154* ⚶

When cutting dough for dinner rolls, use dental floss for a quick and clean cut through bread dough before baking.

⚶ *155* ⚶

Stale bagels, rolls, and muffins can be freshened without a microwave. Sprinkle drops of water on the bread and place in a brown paper bag. Warm in a hot oven for just a few minutes.

⚶ *156* ⚶

Zest up homemade pizza dough. Add dried, crumbled bits of tomato and ¼ t. each of oregano and basil to pizza dough just before kneading.

🦅 *157* 🦅

Add gourmet flair to your next BLT sandwich by adding crumbled bits of fried bacon and dried tomato pieces to your next batch of basic sandwich-bread dough and knead.

🦅 *158* 🦅

High temperatures and overbaking will dry out fish and spoil the flavor. To retain the natural flavor and juices in fresh fish, broil 12 to 15 minutes for 3 lbs. of fish. When baking, test with a fork. Fish will flake easily when done.

🦅 *159* 🦅

Bake potatoes in half the time by placing them in boiling water for 15 minutes before baking in a hot oven.

❧ *160* ❧

Keep sweet potatoes from drying out by oiling the skins with cooking oil before baking.

❧ *161* ❧

Custard will bake evenly without becoming runny when the custard dish is placed in a pan of water.

❧ *162* ❧

Raisins or other dried fruits to be added to cookies, cakes, and breads will be plump and juicy when soaked in warm water for at least 10 minutes before adding to the dough or batter.

🦜 *163* 🦜

Keep raisins, figs, dates, and other dried fruits from lumping all together in your dough or batter by dusting with flour before adding them to the mixture.

🦜 *164* 🦜

When you're using honey in recipes, avoid baking at high temperatures, as it tends to overbrown and scorch.

🦜 *165* 🦜

Muffin batter doesn't require a lot of mixing. Just stir or whisk to blend the ingredients.

🎋 *166* 🎋

Fill muffin cups only three-quarters full to avoid their spilling over the top of the tins when baking.

🎋 *167* 🎋

Not enough batter to fill all the muffin cups on a muffin tin? Fill empty recesses half full of water to prevent scorching.

🎋 *168* 🎋

To save on calories when baking muffins, substitute 2 egg whites for every egg called for in a recipe.

❧ *169* ❧

Dark-coated muffin tins and bread pans brown quicker and bake faster. Decrease the oven temperature by 25°F.

❧ *170* ❧

Set pie pans and casserole dishes on a baking tray before baking in the oven to catch spills and prevent messes.

❧ *171* ❧

Pecan meal is about half the price of pecan pieces. Use it instead in baklava, muffins, breads, tea rings, and other baked goods.

❦ *172* ❦

When it's time to prepare breakfast for a large crew, the easiest way to cook bacon and sausage patties is to bake them in the oven on a jelly-roll pan. The drippings will need to be drained halfway through cooking if you want crisp bacon. After draining the drippings, turn the bacon or sausage over and return to the oven until baked to your liking.

Cooking

Dinnertime. And the living is easy. Sausages are sizzlin'. And the pancakes piled high. What thoughts come to your mind? What familiar sounds do you recollect? Sounds? Yes, the sounds of supper. Back in the days of the wagon trains traveling westward, the chuck wagon's call to "Come and get it" was announced by the ringing of a hand-forged metal triangle bell. Living in the countryside where children have more room to roam, the dinner bell is a welcome sound at mealtime and a necessity for any mother with a soft voice. Country children are taught that at first sound of the ringing bell they are to come to the house. I teach my younger children that they are not to go farther away from the house than the sound of the bell. If they can't hear the bell when I ring it, they are too far away. Mama is usually the one who gets to ring the bell unless a helper is on hand to do so. Guests, too, want to try their hand at ringing the bell. It's an honor, like making a proclamation. For a brief moment you can follow in the footsteps of Paul Revere or some other important historical person who drew eager crowds with his announcement. How else can a child draw such positive attention and cause people to come running?

When our youngest was a baby, he would cry every time he heard a loud noise. I was usually holding him in my arms when it was time to ring the black cast-iron dinner bell mounted on a front porch post. I tried to make the ring as short and sweet as I could, for I knew what was coming next. It came as fast as the ring of the bell. His cry was piercing and probably got the attention of the children playing in the yard more so than the bell. Josiah is now old enough to readily assume the responsibility of sounding the call to dinner himself, vigorously waving back and forth the black leather pull straps attached to the bell. As the years seem to pass too quickly, one day too soon, I fear, he will be on the receiving end of the bell instead of the sending. No longer Mama's right-hand man, he will gladly receive the welcome call to come home from the field, barn, or creek to a hearty meal and time spent together as a family.

The dinner table is a place where each person in the family can join together after a long day of work or study to share and enjoy the company of its members. Children first learn about community events and world issues during these times. It is a view of life and values and priorities gleaned from the wise by the eager ears of the young. Family meal time plays an important part in this parental responsibility. When the table is set attractively and the aroma of spices and herbs fill the air, it is a joy to all to linger long around it. Pleasant discussions and family news is a nightly tradition to look forward to when opportunity is given to everyone to share his or her daily happenings and thoughts. And after everyone has had a chance to converse, an essay, or letter, or scripture is read to further enlighten us all. Dinnertime may very well serve as the most important meal of the day as it feeds our soul.

Supper's ready—hear the bell? It's always nice to be called for dinner. Time to come home and gather around the dinner table once again for a family tradition that needs to be kept alive for the sake of the young and old.

❧ *173* ❧

Social skills and etiquette are best learned around the kitchen table.

❧ *174* ❧

Ever wondered if you added too much seasoning when a recipe calls for a dash? A dash is always less than ⅛ t.!

❧ *175* ❧

Healthier Food Choices
Honey, raw sugar, or stevia instead of white refined sugar.
Brown rice instead of white rice.
Grill, steam, boil, bake, or smoke foods instead of frying.
Whole-grain flours instead of bleached, white flour.
Whole-grain pastas instead of bleached, white pasta.

Pretzels instead of potato chips (especially those with color dyes and MSG).

Sea salt instead of regular table salt.

Lemon juice or apple cider vinegar in place of white vinegar in recipes.

Good water, herbal teas, natural fruit juices, goat's milk, or soy milk instead of soft drinks, caffeine tea, coffee, cow's milk, or sugar-laden beverages.

Romaine lettuce instead of iceberg lettuce.

Dark green vegetables instead of light green.

Tuna and seafood packed in water instead of oil.

Arrowroot and aluminum-free baking powder instead of regular baking powder.

Plain yogurt in place of commercial sour cream.

❧ 176 ❧

Healthier Sugar Substitutes

Refined white sugar has no nutritional value. It's not as healthy a choice as are more natural sweeteners.

1 c. refined white sugar equals

- 1 c. raw sugar
- 1 c. brown sugar

- ½ c. honey
- ½ c. molasses
- ½ c. sorghum
- 1½ c. maple syrup

❧ 177 ❧

To reduce the amount of fat in soups, chicken and dumplings, roasts and gravy, etc., prepare ahead and chill in the refrigerator. The fat will rise to the top and harden. Simply spoon off and discard before reheating.

❧ 178 ❧

Iceberg lettuce has little nutritional value. Try mixing all kinds of greens for your next salad—watercress, clover, chickweed, dandelion, tender beet tops, shredded cabbage, kale, romaine lettuce, and spinach leaves. Many of these salad makings can be gathered from your own garden or found growing wild outdoors in the spring and summer. Much healthier and less expensive when cultivated at home or in the wild.

❧ *179* ❧

Don't discard the outer leaves on a head of lettuce. The darker green leaves on the outside contain the most nutrients.

❧ *180* ❧

To flavor a pot of beans without adding salt or salt pork, season with kelp instead for a healthy substitute.

❧ *181* ❧

Fresh-ground flour contains more than thirty nutrients! After milling, nutrients begin to oxidize. Within about 72 hours, 90 percent of the thirty nutrients are gone. Store fresh-ground flour in the freezer.

❧ *182* ❧

Cooking Substitutions
Vinegar = lemon juice
1 T. cornstarch = 2 T. flour
1 whole egg = 2 egg yolks
1 whole egg = 1 T. water + 2 T. corn oil
1 T. fresh herb = 1 t. dried herb
1 t. dry mustard = 1 T. prepared mustard
1 clove garlic = ⅛ t. garlic powder
1 small onion = 1 T. dried minced onion
¼ t. cream of tartar = 1 t. lemon juice
1 c. commercial sour cream = 1 c. yogurt

🐜 *183* 🐜

If you have a grain mill with metal burrs, you can use it to make homemade peanut butter. (See tip #381.)

🐜 *184* 🐜

Recipe calls for nut halves or pieces? To economize, use peanuts or sunflower seeds instead.

🐜 *185* 🐜

Make your own cornmeal, inexpensively. Buy bulk bags of regular popcorn and grind it!

🦋 *186* 🦋

Grain to Flour or Flakes Measurements
⅔ c. grain = 1 c. flour
1 c. oat groats = 2 c. flakes
3 c. flour = 1 lb. flour, approximately
1 c. rye berries = 2 c. flakes
2¼ c. wheat berries = 1 lb. wheat = approximately 3¾ c. flour
A 6-gallon bucket of wheat berries will yield approximately 158 cups of ground flour!
2½ c. whole corn = 1 lb. corn = 4¼ c. ground cornmeal

🦋 *187* 🦋

Culinary Spices Companion Chart
Beef: Bay leaves, chives, hot peppers, marjoram, oregano, rosemary, peppercorns, savory, thyme
Breads: Anise, caraway, coriander, dill, marjoram, oregano, rosemary, thyme
Pork: Coriander, nutmeg, cumin, garlic, ginger, hot peppers, sage, thyme
Lamb: Garlic, marjoram, oregano, tarragon, mint
Poultry: Rosemary, garlic, sage, chilies, thyme, oregano

❧ *188* ❧

The plastic scoop that comes in boxes of laundry detergent makes a handy rice, flour, grain, or sugar scoop in the kitchen after a thorough wash and rinse. Leave one in each canister or container for convenience.

❧ *189* ❧

Here's how to get all the shortening out of the can. If it's hard to get that last bit out, pour boiling water into the container and the shortening will rise to the surface. Scoop out. Chill to reharden if necessary.

❧ *190* ❧

Never use a can of food with a bulging end. Both ends should be flat. If they're not, discard. Cans with minor dents in the side are okay to use as long as the ends are not bulging. Use these first, since dented cans seem to eventually bulge.

❦ *191* ❦

Wish all the popcorn kernels would pop? Store popcorn in the refrigerator or freezer before popping.

❦ *192* ❦

Never store spices right over the cookstove. The heat and steam will ruin your seasonings.

🦋 *193* 🦋

Need lots of ice for your next dinner party? Make ice cubes ahead of time. As cubes freeze, transfer to a brown paper bag for storage instead of a plastic one and the cubes won't stick together.

🦋 *194* 🦋

Ice-cube trays are great for storing fresh herbs that tend to lose their flavor when dried. Just place the herb leaves in the trays with water and freeze.

🦋 *195* 🦋

Add an attractive and flavorful garnish to your next pitcher of iced tea or lemonade. Freeze fresh leaves of mint, lemon balm, or the peels from lemons, limes, or oranges in ice-cube trays.

❧ 196 ❧

For the punch bowl, garnish with frozen ice rings made with any of the above herbs or peels, or freeze fresh violets, rose petals, or pansies (all are edible) along with a clear or light-colored beverage in a Jell-O mold or muffin tins.

❧ 197 ❧

Bones from smoked meats, especially ham, add rich taste when used to flavor bean or tomato soups.

❧ 198 ❧

Soup too salty? Add chopped raw potatoes while warming. Discard the potatoes, if desired, after enough salt has been absorbed.

🦎 *199* 🦎

Keep a box of dehydrated instant potato flakes on hand to thicken sauces and soups. Potato flakes thicken without masking or changing the flavors. The flakes will take on the flavor of the food they're mixed with.

🦎 *200* 🦎

Have soup once a week. Start a soup or vegetable stew starter pot. Put all leftover meat, vegetables, rice, or potatoes in the soup pot. Store in the refrigerator. On the designated day, add stock and any other vegetables or grains to your pot, cook, and enjoy. The soup starter blend can be stored in the freezer and added to if a larger accumulation of vegetables is needed.

❧ *201* ❧

Plan a smorgasbord-style supper once a week. Save leftover food from several meals in succession and serve once there's enough for everyone to sample a little of many different things. Or each person can have a different entrée. It's a great way to clean out the refrigerator, save on grocery expenses, avoid waste, and give Mom an easy night in the kitchen.

❧ *202* ❧

Have 1 c. of meat left over? Get another meal out of it. Take fish, chicken, turkey, or domestic rabbit and chop into small pieces. Add to a white cream sauce. Serve over biscuit halves or toast points.

❦ 203 ❦

Debone chicken and turkey easily using kitchen scissors instead of a knife.

❦ 204 ❦

Stretch chicken salad by adding chilled, cooked rice.

❦ 205 ❦

Slices of banana bread make great gourmet French toast! (See tip #411.)

☙ 206 ❧

Cauliflower steamed with a wedge of lemon will be less bitter.

☙ 207 ❧

Nobody likes sticky pasta. Add 1 T. of olive or canola oil to the cooking water.

☙ 208 ❧

No need to peel tomatoes when making fresh spaghetti sauce or salsa. Wash the tomatoes well, quarter, and chop in the blender with the skins on.

❦ *209* ❦

Whole tomatoes should be kept at room temperature, not refrigerated.

❦ *210* ❦

Don't let fresh fish or seafood sit at room temperature long. It will spoil in a few hours. Wrap and store in the refrigerator until it's time to cook. Freeze for later use.

❦ *211* ❦

Hard-shell clams are easier to open if boiling water is poured over them.

❦ 212 ❦

Save leftover sweet potatoes from supper. Slice into coins and fry in 1 T. of butter or oil. Great for breakfast, lunch, or anytime.

❦ 213 ❦

One lb. of bacon yields about 1 c. of fat.

❦ 214 ❦

Use fresh meat drippings to make gravy. (See tip #453.) When baking with bacon drippings, use one-quarter less than for other specified shortenings. Fat drippings from beef or pork can be used for soap making. Pour into a jar, add a label with the date, and store in the refrigerator.

❧ 215 ❧

When purchasing bacon, you get more for your money by buying it in ends and pieces.

❧ 216 ❧

Overboil tea? Add a pinch of baking soda immediately to tea to remove the bitter taste.

❧ 217 ❧

Remove the burnt taste from scorched milk by placing the pot in cold water and adding a pinch of salt to the milk.

❦ *218* ❦

When honey hardens and starts to sugar, set the container outdoors under direct sunlight on a sunny, warm day. The honey should return to its natural state, but it may take several days to achieve. Or place honey jar in a double boiler with water. Boil gently until honey thins.

❦ *219* ❦

Not enough ripe tomatoes from the garden to can or make relish or sauce? Whole tomatoes can be frozen as is. Place each tomato in a Ziploc freezer bag and freeze. Add to the collection until you have enough to make the desired condiment.

🦗 *220* 🦗

Buy coffee in bulk for better pricing? Store surplus coffee in a container in the freezer to prolong the fresh flavor and use as needed.

🦗 *221* 🦗

Don't pour leftover coffee down the drain. Make it into iced coffee or pour into ice-cube trays and freeze into cubes to ice future pitchers of iced coffee.

🦗 *222* 🦗

Utilize leftover food in a delicious way. In warmer weather, make stir-fry. In cooler weather, make soup or a casserole. (Use leftover foods such as chopped meat, rice, cabbage, onions, bean sprouts, grated carrots, or whatever else is on hand.)

❦ 223 ❦

To obtain a more subtle flavor when cooking collards, boil them with turkey back, chopped onion, and carrots.

❦ 224 ❦

Turnips cooking on the stove often give off a strong odor. Subdue the odor by adding 1 t. of sugar to the water. It'll enhance the flavor, too.

❦ 225 ❦

If lettuce is sparse in late winter and early spring, grow sprouts in a jar and hunt chickweed outdoors. Chickweed is considered a weed by many and pops up in lawns everywhere. However, it's an herb, high in vitamin C, and when combined with bean sprouts makes a tasty salad. Serve with your favorite dressing.

🦋 *226* 🦋

Maple syrup can be substituted for granulated sugar in most recipes. Use 1½ c. maple syrup for each 1 c. of granulated sugar. Add ¼ t. soda for each cup of syrup used as well.

🦋 *227* 🦋

To soften hardened brown sugar, place the amount needed in a pan in the oven at 300°F for 15 minutes.

🦋 *228* 🦋

Chopped green tomatoes make a great substitute for chopped bell peppers in casseroles, omelets, and other recipes.

❧ *229* ☙

Hard, aged cheeses are best made in spring and late autumn when it is cooler, thus preventing mold formation on the cheese surface.

❧ *230* ☙

Need a cheese press? Here's a handy substitute. Lay the fresh cheese block on a plate. Place a second plate on top, bottom side against the cheese. Weigh down with 10-lb. bags of flour or sugar for the appropriate length of time. Drain off any liquid that accumulates.

❧ *231* ☙

Never use an aluminum pot when making cheese or soap. Reserve aluminum cookware for candle making.

❧ *232* ❧

It is important to chill fresh raw milk as soon as possible to ensure the fresh taste. Always strain milk from the milk pail to a sterile jar, then place immediately into cold water or the refrigerator.

❧ *233* ❧

To separate cream from milk, pour fresh raw milk into a clean, wide-mouth glass jar and refrigerate. Undisturbed, the cream will rise to the top. Dip it out with a ladle. Use the cream to make butter. (See tip #371.)

❧ *234* ❧

You can get more cream out of milk by heating the milk until lukewarm, then chilling it quickly.

❧ 235 ❧

If cream is starting to taste sour, restore its sweetness by adding a pinch of baking soda.

❧ 236 ❧

When you're making yogurt at home, cow's milk works best. When using goat's milk, add some dry powdered milk to help it thicken. Or add a little gelatin, and the yogurt will resemble the store-bought cultures.

❧ 237 ❧

Set the butter dish on top of the stove while you cook so it will soften by the time dinner is served.

❦ *238* ❦

Homemade butter gone sour? Don't throw it out! Mix powdered garlic and salt with slightly soured butter for a delicious garlic-toast spread.

❦ *239* ❦

Buttermilk adds splendid flavor to corn bread and makes homemade bread more tender.

❦ *240* ❦

Buttermilk can be used as a starter in cheese making.

❦ 241 ❦

If you don't have buttermilk on hand, add 2 T. of lemon juice or vinegar to 2 c. of sweet milk and stir.

❦ 242 ❦

The best knife for slicing tomatoes is a serrated bread knife.

🦋 243 🦋

Problem with ice-cream cones dripping? Before adding the ice cream, place a mini marshmallow or a bit of marshmallow creme in the bottom of the cone.

🦋 244 🦋

To help beans soften when cooking on the stove top, do not add salt to the water. Wait and season once the beans are almost done.

🦋 245 🦋

When draining off the juice from cans of pineapple and other fruits, pour into Popsicle molds and freeze for a cool and refreshing treat.

⚜ 246 ⚜

To determine whether an egg is fresh, place it in a glass of water. A fresh egg will sink in water.

⚜ 247 ⚜

Oops! Cracked an egg you were about to boil? It can still be boiled. Just add 1 t. of salt to boiling water, then add the egg. The contents will not ooze out. The salt will cause the egg white to set more quickly.

⚜ 248 ⚜

No eggs for baking? Here's a substitute. For every whole egg a recipe calls for, add 1 T. of water and 2 T. of corn oil.

❦ 249 ❧

The easiest way to separate egg yolks from whites is to crack the shell and drop the egg into your palm. Allow the whites to pass through your fingers.

❦ 250 ❧

It's easiest to separate egg yolks from whites when the eggs are cold.

❦ 251 ❧

Eggshells peel most easily from hard-boiled eggs while they're still hot. Quickly rinse in cold water first.

❧ 252 ❧

Perfect poached eggs can be had with this French secret. Add 1 T. of vinegar and some salt to the water. Stir the boiling water with a spoon until a whirlpool forms in the center. Slip the egg from a saucer into the whirlpool and continue to stir gently until the egg is cooked to your liking.

❧ 253 ❧

Egg yolks can be kept fresh in the refrigerator for several days when covered with cold water.

❧ 254 ❧

To prevent eggs from cracking when hard boiling, place them in very warm water first and allow to come to a boil slowly.

🦋 255 🦋

When pieces of broken eggshell fall into the bowl of eggs, scoop them out with a large piece of eggshell. Works like a magnet!

🦋 256 🦋

It takes about seven or eight egg whites to make 1 c.

🦋 257 🦋

Rinse all fresh vegetables and greens in water before preparing, but do not soak in water for long periods of time. Soaking in water will dissolve the minerals, thus reducing the nutrient content.

❧ *258* ☙

Cook vegetables only until tender when forked. Keep the pot covered during cooking to preserve as many vitamins as possible.

❧ *259* ☙

Pea pods can be used to add flavor to soup stock.

❧ *260* ☙

Oatmeal flakes can be used to thicken soups.

🎋 *261* 🎋

Add pizzazz to fried oysters by rolling them in cracker crumbs mixed with 1 t. of celery salt before frying.

🎋 *262* 🎋

Homemade doughnuts won't absorb grease when 1 T. of vinegar is added to the frying pot.

🎋 *263* 🎋

When serving cold soup, make it the day before and re-frigerate. Chill the bowls in the refrigerator hours before serving as well.

❧ 264 ❧

Day-old and older breads make better toast than fresh bread.

❧ 265 ❧

When keeping lettuce in the refrigerator, place it in a paper towel or nonprinted newsprint.

❧ 266 ❧

The skin on beets can be removed easily when they're brought to a boil, then dipped in cold water.

❧ 267 ❧

To preserve the white color of cauliflower, soak for 30 minutes in cold, salted water before cooking.

❧ 268 ❧

Eyes tear when peeling onions? Hold the onion under cold running water while peeling.

❧ 269 ❧

Mashed potatoes will look like whipped cream if hot milk is added to them before mashing.

❧ 270 ❧

Add too much milk to mashed potatoes? Thicken with cream cheese. Whip to combine.

❧ 271 ❧

Rice will not get mushy if cooked in water with 1 t. of lemon juice added for each qt. of water.

❧ 272 ❧

Keep freshly chopped fruits from discoloring while you prepare fruit salad by pouring a little orange juice or lemon juice over them.

❧ 273 ❧

Before juicing oranges and lemons, grate the rind for use as a flavoring in cookies, pies, cakes, crêpes, pancakes, muffins, etc.

❧ 274 ❧

Juices from canned or cooked vegetables and fruits are rich in vitamins and flavor. Don't throw them out. Store in a glass jar in the refrigerator, one jar for fruit juices and one jar for a vegetable blend. Either can stretch store-bought juice. Juices can also be mixed with baby cereal to add extra nutrients to the older baby/toddler's diet. Vegetable liquids can also be used in a soup base.

❧ 275 ❧

To get the most juice out of a lemon, orange, or tanger-ine, place it in hot water for several minutes before juicing it.

❧ 276 ❧

Gently roll citrus fruit on a tabletop or in the palm of your hand to warm and soften before squeezing to get more juice out.

❧ 277 ❧

Need to sweeten your iced tea a little more? Squeeze the juice from an orange wedge into your glass. It's nat-urally sweet and full of good flavor.

🐦 *278* 🐦

Don't use a fork to turn chicken or rabbit when baking, grilling, or frying. It will pierce the meat and let the juices escape. Use tongs instead to keep the meat juicier.

🐦 *279* 🐦

To prevent steaks or chops from curling when broiling or frying, score the edges of the fat with a knife every one to two inches.

🐦 *280* 🐦

Skillets and griddles don't need greasing if the batter includes fat.

❦ 281 ❦

To lightly grease a skillet or griddle, rub with a potato half. It won't smoke like oil or shortening.

❦ 282 ❦

When making pancakes, waffles, French toast, or biscuits, double the batch. Store the abundance in the refrigerator for another meal the same week. Or freeze for use on sick days or when longer breakfast preparation time is not in the schedule.

❦ 283 ❦

Many wonderful gifts can be crafted in the kitchen. Try making your own gift baskets filled with homemade jellies and jams, muffins, bread, herbed vinegar, relishes, pickles, cheese balls, or herbal teas right off your pantry shelves. Spruce up canning jars with round doilies or calico placed under the band. Or tie on with raffia and garnish with a dried orange slice or cinnamon sticks. Perfect, practical gifts for everyone on your gift list.

🌾 284 🌾

Make your own homespun recipe cards. With pinking shears, cut heart shapes from calico fabric and glue to the corner of index cards. Tie together with raffia a dozen cards containing your favorite recipes, make a raffia bow, and you'll have another gift from the kitchen. Perfect gift idea for the new bride.

Food Storage and Preserving

Harvest on the homestead. A time to reap the bounty of the harvest. A time to count your abundance and blessings. A time to give thanks. A time to pick and clean and peel and pare and chop and slice and pickle and preserve and simmer and dry and freeze and can. A time to gather with family and friends and share the work and share the wealth of natural resources. Work now will save much later.

One of the most beautiful sights to behold in the South is a pecan orchard in the wintertime or early spring when the leaves have all fallen away and the beautiful bare branches of the trees afford an unobstructed view. The stately pecan is native to North America and was introduced to the European settlers in addition to corn and the turkey by the Native Americans.

We had the privilege of having such a tree on our suburban lot in north Florida. During some harvests, the squirrels consumed the majority of the pecans. Squirrels are difficult to combat because they aren't quite as finicky as we are. Squirrels don't wait until the pecans are ready to harvest. They will eat them green or at least remove them from the tree before they're fully matured. We felt they knew they were winning the race to the pecans as they sat smugly on the lofty branches nibbling away, while staring us straight in the eye! To top it all off, squirrels are terribly wasteful. They remove a pecan, take a bite or two, then throw it to the ground. We were bombarded by the dislodged shells of the squirrel brigade as we walked from the front door to the driveway.

Here in Tennessee we have walnut trees instead. When the walnuts fall from the trees, you'd better stand clear. A bop on the head from a falling walnut is one you won't soon forget. We learned from the locals to lay the black walnuts out on the driveway as soon as they fall from the trees, so our truck or van can run over them to crack the hard outer hull. Once the hull is removed, we gather them up. Last season we gathered at least six huge buckets full. So guess what we gave at Thanksgiving? You guessed right. A bucket of walnuts and a trusty surefire nutcracker. Sharing the bounty and giving thanks to God. It's a vital part of harvesttime on our homestead.

❦ *285* ❦

Peaches ripen quickly if placed in a box covered with newspaper.

❦ *286* ❦

Corn oil keeps longer at room temperature than any other vegetable oil.

❦ *287* ❦

Dampen the rim of a bowl or jar so the plastic storage wrap will cling better in the refrigerator.

☙ 288 ☙

To save on cling wraps, cover bowls with elasticized shower caps.

☙ 289 ☙

Before preparing purchased fruits and vegetables, wash them in a solution of apple cider vinegar and water to remove any pesticide or chemical residue. Allow to soak for a few minutes in the solution before rinsing under tap water.

☙ 290 ☙

It is important to wash the rind before slicing purchased pumpkin, watermelon, cantaloupe, and the like or the presence of any pesticides will be transferred to the knife and then into the flesh of the fruit as it's sliced.

🦋 *291* 🦋

Keep cheese fresh in the refrigerator longer. Store with a sugar cube to prevent mold formation.

🦋 *292* 🦋

Bananas too ripe to eat? Place directly into the freezer, peel and all, to store. Keep adding bananas until enough is acquired to make banana bread or another recipe. Remove when ready to use, peel, and mash the bananas with a fork.

🦋 *293* 🦋

Freeze fish and poultry like the professionals. Place fresh meat whole or in cuts on a tray and place in the freezer until frozen (one day). Remove from the freezer and dip in a pot of cold water. Return to the freezer. The ice glaze will protect it from drying out.

❧ *294* ❧

Thaw frozen fish in a pan of milk.

❧ *295* ❧

To retain the vitamins, don't cut the caps off of strawberries before freezing.

❧ *296* ❧

Don't wash fresh blueberries before freezing. Wash just before eating.

⚜ 297 ⚜

The key to storing pecan meats for extended periods of time is keeping them at low temperatures. Shelled pecans kept on the pantry shelf will remain fresh for only two months and are susceptible to insect invasions. In the refrigerator, pecans may keep for more than nine months. In the freezer, at 0°F, pecans can be retained for two years or more. Pecans freeze well and suffer no loss of quality when frozen. They may be defrosted and refrozen again and again due to their low moisture content (4 percent) without affecting on the quality or texture of the meat.

⚜ 298 ⚜

Don't discard celery tops. The leafy tops are edible, adding lots of tasty flavor to soups, stews, relishes, and roasts. Dehydrate in a warm oven and store in an airtight container.

🦎 *299* 🦎

Keep fresh asparagus and celery stalks from wilting in the refrigerator. Store upright in a tall drinking glass one-third full of water.

🦎 *300* 🦎

Prevent the spoilage of greens and other vegetables in the crisper section of your refrigerator. Line the compartment with paper towels or print-free newspaper to absorb the excess moisture.

🦎 *301* 🦎

Don't wash newly collected farm eggs before storing. Water destroys the protective film that keeps out air, bacteria, and odors. Wash them just before you're ready to use them.

ೠ *302* ೠ

Process your own meat chickens? Keep the birds in cool water after scalding. Add cider vinegar to the water in the holding tank (ice chest, tub, etc.) to keep down bacterial growth during processing.

ೠ *303* ೠ

All freshly slaughtered meat should be immediately chilled. Place it in a cooler with water and ice to lower the temperature before processing.

ೠ *304* ೠ

When you're dressing tough old birds (hens or roosters) or rabbits, grind the meat, then pressure-can it. Use the meat in casseroles, barbecue, or salads. Pressure-can in quart canning jars with water and 1 t. salt at 10 lbs. pressure for 90 minutes.

🐉 *305* 🐉

To remove excess air from plastic storage bags of foods about to be frozen, place a drinking straw in the corner and close the bag up to the straw. Draw in a deep breath using the straw to remove excess air. Quickly pull out the straw and seal the bag.

🐉 *306* 🐉

In case of a power outage, do not open the freezer. The food should stay frozen about two days. If the freezer is not running after that time, add dry ice. If that's not available, consider canning the meat and most valuable contents. No need to let it all spoil.

❦ *307* ❦

Never rely totally on electricity for preserving your food. Keep a gas stove or propane fish cooker on hand for canning and cooking during power outages.

❦ *308* ❦

Save empty glass containers such as pickle and mayonnaise jars for storage of dried herbs, rice, beans, and sprouting seeds. Glass containers can even be used for freezing.

❦ *309* ❦

Empty mayonnaise jars can be reused for water-bath canning.

☙ *310* ❧

Water-bath canning and pressure-canning make good use of the energy consumed. How else can you prepare seven meals at once with the same amount of fuel consumed to prepare just one? I call it a homesteaders' "dinner in a jar" or "fast food in a jar." There's no thawing time. You can enjoy it right out of the jar or heat and serve. And the jars look pretty on your pantry shelves, too!

☙ *311* ❧

Before canning, carefully examine each jar. Run your finger around the rim to check for nicks. The rim should be smooth. Also look for cracks in the jar itself. If any chips or cracks are noticed, discard the jar.

🦋 *312* 🦋

Use your oven to heat and sterilize canning jars. Put clean jars into the oven at the lowest possible setting for 30 minutes. Remove and fill with hot food product.

🦋 *313* 🦋

Always wipe the rim of each canning jar with a clean napkin or cloth before affixing lids and rings.

🦋 *314* 🦋

For the best homemade pickles, select freshly picked cucumbers and pickle within 24 hours.

❧ *315* ❧

It is recommended that all home-canned meats and vegetables be brought to a boil before tasting.

❧ *316* ❧

All seafood, poultry, meats, and low-acid vegetables may be home-canned without adding salt. Salt serves only as a seasoning.

❧ *317* ❧

In canning, sugar helps to retain the fruits' natural color and adds sweetness. Yet it is not necessary to add a sugar syrup or sweetener when canning fruits and fruit juices. Sugar does not prevent or retard spoilage. If a sugar-free product is desired, add boiling water or natural fruit juice instead.

❦ *318* ❦

After apples and other fruits have been peeled and cored, try this to prevent browning. Place the fruit in a bowl and cover with water. Add a couple of tablespoons of lemon juice, orange juice, or a crushed vitamin C tablet (ascorbic acid).

❦ *319* ❦

When canning starchy vegetables such as peas, corn, lima beans, and potatoes, leave a 1" headspace when filling the jars. These foods expand during the canning process.

❦ *320* ❦

Canning-jar lids can be reused if they're removed without damage by a canning-jar lid opener. Check the lid before reusing to make sure it will give a good seal.

🦋 *321* 🦋

Canning is often done in summer when summer crops are harvested. To keep from heating the house in hot weather, can outdoors on a gas fish cooker. It heats up faster than a conventional stove. Most modern stoves are not built to endure the weight or the heat of canners with filled jars and water.

🦋 *322* 🦋

When removing the jars from a canner, allow to cool naturally at room temperature, away from any draft. Never place them in cold water to hurry the process.

🦋 *323* 🦋

Always remove canning rings from the jars to test the lids for a firm seal before storing on pantry shelves. If any jars did not seal, use the contents promptly, store in the refrigerator and use within the week, or freeze.

❧ *324* ❧

Hospitality in a jar. A welcome gift to receive is a box of jars filled with home-canned goodies. Give to a new neighbor as a welcome or a friend packing up to move. Keep a student from starving while away at school by providing home-cooked meals in a jar.

❦ *325* ❧

Concord grapes make the sweetest, best grape jelly.

❦ *326* ❧

Flavored vinegar is popular due to its many culinary attributes. It can be used as a condiment, as a food seasoning, as a preservative, as a marinade, and of course in salad dressings.

❦ *327* ❧

Fruits blend well with white wine and apple cider vinegars, which are fruity as well.

❦ *328* ❦

Herbs and spices complement red wine and white distilled vinegar.

❦ *329* ❦

When making flavored vinegar, use only fresh fruits, herbs, and spices. The fresher the ingredients, the more intense the flavor will be.

❦ *330* ❦

A general rule to use when making flavored vinegar is about 1 c. of fresh herbs and/or spices to 2 c. of vinegar. Fruit-flavored vinegar takes about 1 c. of fruit to 1 c. of vinegar.

☼ *331* ☼

Be sure that those attractive bottles selected to house homemade flavored vinegar have been washed thoroughly in hot soapy water and then rinsed well in boiling water. The fruits and/or herbs should also be fresh, rinsed in cool water, and free of debris or spoilage.

☼ *332* ☼

Try these combinations when making your own flavored vinegar at home:

Apple cider vinegar with mint.

Red wine vinegar with basil and garlic.

White wine vinegar with orange rind and rosemary.

Food Preservation Recipes

🦋 *333* 🦋

There are three basic methods of preparing flavored vinegar. Merely add a sprig of your desired herb or fruit to the vinegar and allow to sit for a week or two, steep either herbs or fruit in simmering vinegar, or heat vinegar and pour it into a bottle containing your choice of herb or fruit flavorings.

🦋 *334* 🦋

Strawberry-Apple Vinegar
Yield: 1 pt.
4 medium strawberries, fresh
1 t. lemon juice
1 pt. apple cider vinegar
Squeeze the strawberries and their juice into one pint-size bottle. Add the lemon juice and vinegar. Cover, shake, and, if desired, strain after ten to fourteen days.

☙ 335 ❧

Freezing Fresh Lemon Juice

If you're blessed with a lemon tree, preserve some fresh lemon juice to have year-round. Juice lemons and pour into ice-cube trays. (Dry the peels for later recipes.) Once frozen, remove from the trays and store in a freezer bag. Each cube will yield about 2 T. of lemon juice. Remove as needed for recipes.

☙ 336 ❧

Freezing Eggs for Storage

Have an abundance of eggs? Break each egg open one at a time. Inspect for freshness, then beat lightly. Place one egg into each compartment of an oiled ice-cube tray. Freeze. Once frozen, store in Ziploc bags. Remove as many as your recipe prescribes. Allow to thaw before use in baking. Eggs can be kept in the freezer up to one year.

❧ *337* ❧

Storing Fresh Farm Eggs Without Refrigeration
Store whole eggs in the shell just like the old farmers did before refrigerators. Eggs will keep for a year! Coat fresh whole eggs with a thick coating of lard. Pack into a large bucket with plenty of salt. Add more salt as you add more eggs. Affix the lid and write the date of the eggs on top. Store the egg bucket in a cool place, out of direct sunlight. The cooler the temperature, the better. A cool root cellar is ideal for long-term storage of whole eggs.

❧ *338* ❧

Dehydrating Wheat Grass
Keep wheat grass on hand all year round. When weather permits, grow a small bed of wheat grass, clip, and dry. Dehydrate in a gas oven on a tray, in an electric oven at 150°F, or in a dehydrator. Once dry, pulverize into powder and store in jars for the winter months. (See tip #393 for growing wheat grass.)

❊ 339 ❊

Dried Tomatoes

Tomatoes, herbs, and bell peppers can be dried in a gas oven without turning on the heat. The pilot light is enough to dry them adequately. Slice firm tomatoes or peppers and place on a broiler tray (one with a slotted top to allow air flow and drainage). Place the tray on a roasting pan to catch any liquid. Most herbs will dry overnight.

Or dry in an electric oven at 150°F. Store dehydrated herbs and vegetables in a dry container out of direct sunlight to prevent mold formation.

❊ 340 ❊

Corncob Syrup

Save those corncobs to make a wonderful maple syrup substitute. Great on pancakes, waffles, and French toast.

Take approximately 24 cobs minus the corn, break in half, and again into fourths. Place in a kettle, cover with water, and boil for 2 hours. Keep the corncobs covered with water throughout the process. Add hot water as needed. Remove the cobs; strain the liquid. Then boil down to half. Add 1 c. of sugar or ½ c. of honey for every cup of liquid left in the pot. Boil down to your desired thickness and add a pinch of cream of tartar. Pour into glass jars while hot and seal.

Stores on the shelf long term. If refrigerated, the syrup will thicken to butter/spread consistency and will not pour easily.

Recipe adapted from Countryside *magazine*

❦ *341* ❦

Storing Butter in Saltwater Brine
Fill a sterilized gallon jug container (glass, stoneware, or plastic) three-quarters full of fresh, cool water. Add 1 c. of canning salt or other plain salt (without iodine) and dissolve. Place an uncooked egg into the container to test the brine. If the egg floats, the brine is salty enough to preserve butter. If it does not, remove the egg, add more salt, and dissolve. Continue testing until the egg floats. Remove the egg. Add fresh butter and cover. Store the

butter brine in a cellar, basement, springhouse, or un-heated, cool room. Remove butter as needed.

☙ 342 ☙

Vegetable Stew (Pressure-Canning Recipe)
Yield: Approximately 15 qts.
Wash and prepare the following fresh raw vegetables:
2 gals. tomatoes, quartered
2 to 2½ dozen potatoes, chopped
3 qts. carrots, coined
2 bunches celery, chopped
2 large onions, chopped
6 crookneck squash or zucchini, chopped
2 heads cabbage, shredded
3 bell peppers, chopped
4 cloves garlic

Heat 5 qts. water to boiling and stir in ½ c. sea salt and 1 t. cayenne or pepper.

Place the vegetable stew mix into hot quart jars, leaving a 1" headspace. Fill the remainder of the jar with boiling water.

Pressure-can at 10 lbs. pressure for 30 minutes.

Note: Perfect companion to beef stew. Recipe doubles easily. Just mix the chopped vegetables in a clean, food-grade bucket or ice chest and stir with a long-handled spoon. After using this recipe once, you will be able to improvise and select a combination of chopped vegetables to suit your family. Use more or less of the vegetables you prefer.

🐲 343 🐲

Chili Beans (Pressure Canning Recipe)
Yield: 17 to 18 qts.
10 lbs. pinto or kidney beans
4 c. bell pepper, chopped
7 c. onions, chopped
10 to 20 oz. Worcestershire sauce
¼ c. garlic powder
⅔ c. chili powder
½ c. salt
1½ c. brown sugar
¼ c. dry mustard
6 chili peppers, seeded and diced (optional)
Soak the 10 lbs. of beans overnight covered with water. Afterward, drain off the water.

Bring 7 qts. of water to a boil.

While the water is heating, add the drained beans and remaining ingredients to a huge pot (water-bath canner size). Add the boiling water to the huge pot and stir through to the bottom to mix. Bring all to a boil. Allow the mixture to boil for 5 minutes on medium-high heat. Immediately fill quart jars with the chili bean mix, leaving a 1" headspace. Run a rubber spatula down the insides of each jar to release any air pockets and to ensure a complete filling. Wipe the tops clean and seal with lids and bands. Process the jars of chili beans in a pressure canner at 10 lbs. pressure for 65 minutes.

Note: The beans will be fully cooked. To use, remove from the jar and reheat. (See tips #443, 444, 454, and 455 for serving suggestions.)

❧ *344* ❧

Pork and Beans (Pressure-Canning Recipe)
Yield: 4 qts.

Soak 3 lbs. of dried navy beans in plenty of water overnight. Drain and rinse the beans in the morning and pour into a pot along with 3 pts. of barbecue sauce (see tip #355) and 1 pt. of water. Heat through until boiling. Place one-half slice of raw bacon and 1 T. of finely chopped onion in each quart canning jar and pour hot beans and sauce on top. (Each jar will need enough liquid in it to cover the beans. Leave a 2" to 3" headspace at the top to allow for expansion.) Seal with lids and rings and pressure-can at 10 lbs. pressure for 90 minutes. Check to ensure that the jars are sealed, and store on pantry shelves until ready to use.

To use: Open one or two quart jars of baked beans and bacon and warm in a pot on the stove top. If the beans appear a little dry, add water, as much as needed. Stir in additional seasonings and sauce (such as honey and ketchup) if desired to thicken and serve or pour into a casserole dish and bake in the oven for 45 minutes to 1 hour.

❧ 345 ❧

Baby Lima Beans (Pressure-Canning Recipe)
Yield: 7 qts.

Soak 4 lbs. of beans in water overnight. Drain off the water and rinse in the morning. Place the beans in quart canning jars until almost full, leaving a 1" to 2" head-space. Pour boiling water into the hot jars and add 1 t. canning salt to each jar. Top with lids and rings and pressure-can at 10 lbs. pressure for 90 minutes.

❧ 346 ❧

Great Northern Beans (Pressure-Canning Recipe)
Yield: 5 qts.

Soak 3 lbs. of dried beans in water overnight. The next morning, drain and rinse the beans. Add 1 t. salt to each quart jar and spoon in the beans. Pour boiling water into each jar to cover the beans. Leave 1" to 2" head space. Pressure-can at 10 lbs. pressure for 90 minutes.

To use: Empty the contents of a quart jar into a pan on the stove and reheat. Add a little water if the gravy is thicker than desired. If serving over rice, don't combine the cooked rice and beans in the same pot when heating, as the rice has a tendency to soak up the natural juices from the beans.

🦎 *347* 🦎

Preserved Brown Rice (Pressure-Canning Recipe)
In quart canning jars, add ¼ to ½ c. of brown rice and 1 t. of canning salt. Fill to 2" from the top with either hot water or hot chicken broth. Fill enough jars to make one canner load. Pressure-can at 10 lbs. pressure for 60 minutes.

To use: Drain off the water if adding to casseroles. Pour into a pot and heat on the stove when making chicken and rice or soup.

Variation: Add a couple of chopped tomatoes to the jar, along with salt, brown rice, and plenty of water. Perfect starter base for gumbo. Add seasonings as desired.

🦎 348 🦎

Barbecue Pork (Pressure-Canning Instructions)

The key to obtaining the best flavor is to first smoke the meat. Start with a large, fresh pork harm. If it's not smoked, smoke in a charcoal smoker according to manufacturer's directions until done. Be sure to add some hickory chips in with the charcoal. Remember, smoked meat has a pink tint to it even when fully cooked. When it's cool enough to handle, cut the meat into chunks and place in quart canning jars. To each jar add 2 to 3 drops of Liquid Smoke and 1 t. of salt. Fill the jars with water up to 1" from the threaded top. Wipe jar rims with a clean paper napkin and affix canning lids and bands. Pressure-can at 10 lbs. of pressure for 90 minutes.

To serve: Add the contents of a quart jar to a pot and heat. Once hot, drain off the water. Add your favorite barbecue sauce, stir, and serve.

✹ 349 ✹

Canned Meat: Venison, Beef, Pork, Rabbit, Goat, and Poultry (Pressure-Canning Recipe)
If you think that deer meat is too tough and chewy for your palate, try canning your next deer. Canning tenderizes meat tremendously. Place ground meat or chunks after rinsing in cool water in quart canning jars. Add water and 1 t. salt and pressure-can for 90 minutes at 10 lbs. pressure.

✹ 350 ✹

Free Dog Food (Pressure-Canning Recipe)
When butchering time rolls around, don't forget to save the scraps (deer, goat, beef, or pork) that won't be used for human consumption. Scraps can be used for dog food. Place in canning jars, fill with water, and pressure-can at 10 lbs. pressure for 90 minutes.

❦ *351* ❧

Canned Bulk Pork Sausage (Pressure-Canning Recipe)
To can bulk sausage, place 1 lb. bulk sausage, uncooked, into a sterilized canning jar with 1 t. salt, and add some water. Pressure-can at 10 lbs. pressure for 90 minutes.

To use: Drain off the water and fry until browned in a skillet on the stove top. Use in casseroles, omelets, scrambled eggs, etc. (See tips #402, 410, 450, and 451 for serving suggestions.)

❦ *352* ❧

Canned Sausage Patties (Pressure-Canning Recipe)
Shape bulk sausage into patties and fry until three-quarters done. For large quantities, shape patties and bake on trays in the oven until three-quarters done. Layer the sausage patties in wide-mouth quart canning jars. Pour ¼ c. of the sausage drippings into each jar. Seal with lids and rings and pressure-can at 10 lbs. pressure for 90 minutes.

From the kitchen of Arlene Nyhoff

🜁 *353* 🜁

Honey Mustard Slaw (Water-Bath Canning Recipe)
Yield: 5 pts.
3 carrots, grated
2 large onions, chopped
2 large bell peppers, chopped (for added color use 1 red
    and 1 yellow or orange)
2 c. prepared mustard
2 c. apple cider vinegar
1½ c. honey
2 t. black pepper
2 t. sea salt
1 gal. grated cabbage
Combine all the ingredients except the cabbage in a large
pot and cook on low to medium heat for 15 minutes.
Then add the grated cabbage, stirring to combine, and
cook an additional 5 minutes. Bring the mixture to a boil
and pack into hot, sterilized canning jars. Wipe the jar
rims clean and affix lids and rings. Water-bath can pint
jars in boiling water for 15 minutes.

Note: If you want to make a batch to serve instead of
preserve, reduce the recipe proportions by one-half.
Refrigerate any leftover slaw or unsealed jars.

Adapted from the kitchen of Annette Godwin

✂ 354 ✂

Deborah's Own Honey Barbecue Sauce (Water-Bath Canning Recipe)
Yield: 3 pts.
4 c. tomato puree (process fresh tomatoes in a blender)
1 t. minced garlic
4 T. brown sugar
½ c. honey
½ t. cumin
2 T. Mrs. Dash seasoning
4 T. prepared mustard
8 t. flour
1 c. apple cider vinegar
1½ to 2 t. Worcestershire sauce
1 t. Liquid Smoke
1 T. sea salt
3 t. turmeric
2 t. ground dry mustard
Mix all ingredients together in a large pot on the stove and heat to boiling. Turn to medium heat, stirring occasionally for 5 minutes. Pack into hot sterilized canning jars, leaving a ½" headspace. Cap with hot lids and rings and process in a boiling-water-bath canner for 15 minutes after the water returns to a boil.

❧ *355* ❧

Spiced Oranges or Tangerines (Water-Bath Canning Recipe)
Yield: 6 pts. or 3 qts.
8 oranges or tangerines
3 c. raw sugar
1 c. light brown sugar
4 c. water
½ c. apple cider vinegar
10 whole cloves
1 cinnamon stick
Simmer the whole oranges or tangerines in a pot of water until the skins pierce easily with a fork (approximately 15 to 20 minutes). Remove the oranges from the pot and quarter. (If using small oranges, halve.) Heat the sugar, water, and vinegar in a pot to a boil. Tie the spices in a clean muslin bag and drop into the boiling pot along with the quartered fruit. Reduce the heat and allow to simmer for 30 minutes. Remove the spice bag and pour the hot spiced oranges and juice into pint canning jars. Seal the jars with lids and rings and boil in a hot-water bath for 10 minutes. Remove and store in the pantry once the jars have sealed and cooled. (See tip #386 for a serving suggestion.)

❧ 356 ❧

Pickled Eggs (Water-Bath Canning Recipe)
Great way to preserve an abundance of eggs.

Chop and add to your favorite potato salad dish or grate into tuna salad.

Here's how: Bring 3 c. water to a boil. Stir in 3 c. white vinegar and 6 T. canning salt. Add a sprig of dill or some dill seeds to each canning jar. Fill the canning jars with peeled hard-boiled eggs. A quart jar will hold about a dozen eggs. Pour in the pickling solution and seal with lids and rings. Water-bath can in boiling water for 20 minutes.

From the kitchen of Ann Meeks

❧ 357 ❧

Canning Fresh Blueberries (Water-Bath Canning Recipe)
Place blueberries in an old pillowcase or construct a simple muslin or cheesecloth bag and tie closed. Blanch blueberries in boiling water for 30 seconds or until spots appear on the cloth bag. Plunge into a deep pan of cold

water for 30 seconds, then fill sterilized canning jars. Add some water, leaving a 1" headspace in the jar.

Water-bath can pint jars for 15 minutes and quart jars for 20 minutes.

From the kitchen of Ginger McNeil

(See tips #403 and 404 for making blueberry syrup and pancakes.)

❧ *358* ❧

Grape Juice (Water-Bath Canning Recipe)
Into a sterile quart jar, add: 1 heaping cup of Concord grapes, rinsed, and ½ c. of raw sugar (optional). Fill jars with boiling water, leaving a ¼" headspace at the top before putting on lids and rings. Process in a hot-water bath for 15 minutes. Remove and allow to cool naturally. Store on a pantry shelf or box for at least two months before using. Strain and chill before serving.

Note: Add more or less sugar according to your preference, or omit the sugar altogether.

From the kitchen of Brenda Jane Falk

✵ *359* ✵

Canned Milk (Pressure-Canning Recipe)
No need to buy powdered or canned milk for use in cooking and baking when you have a dairy goat or cow. Just place the milk in pint or quart canning jars with lids and rings and pressure-can at 10 lbs. pressure for 20 minutes. Stock up extra jars to have during dry times!

Serving suggestion: Use in any cooking recipe in which milk is specified.

✵ *360* ✵

Canned Butter
Heat glass canning jars (pint or ½-pint size) in a 250°F oven for 20 minutes, without lids or rings. While the jars are heating, melt butter in a deep saucepan (do not fill more than halfway) slowly until it reaches a boil. Reduce the heat to a simmer and cover. Simmer for 5 minutes. (Watch carefully; if the pot boils over, you'll have a fire!) Pour melted butter into the hot jars through a canning funnel. Do not fill the jars more than three-quarters full

to allow for slight expansion as the butter cools and returns to a solid. Wipe the jar rims with a clean cloth and seal with lids and rings. Once the jars have cooled, put in the refrigerator to harden the butter. Then remove the rings and test each lid for a tight seal. Sealed jars can be stored in the pantry.

From the kitchen of Sylvia Britton

🐦 *361* 🐦

How to Prepare Fresh Pumpkin

Cut a pumpkin in half and then into fourths, if working on a large pumpkin. Use a large spoon or scoop to remove the seeds, and set aside. (Seeds are edible and nutritious, too. Save for roasting.) Place the pumpkin skin-side down in a roasting pan. Add a little water to cover the bottom of the pan and cover. Place in a 300°F oven. The pumpkin will take about 1 hour, unless you are working with a small one. Test the center for softness with a knife. When done, it will slice easily. Remove from the oven when it's ready and uncover. Allow to cool slightly to the touch. Cut the fleshy part away from the hard outside shell. Chop into 2" to 3" chunks. If the pumpkin will be used solely for breads or pies, process the pumpkin cubes in a blender or food processor until smooth. Store long term by freezing in storage bags or pressure-can in pint canning jars.

❧ 362 ❧

Roasted Pumpkin Seeds
Hand-rub pumpkin seeds in a bowl of water to remove the pumpkin. Dry the seeds on a towel and coat lightly with cooking oil (or melted butter) and salt. Place on a cookie sheet and bake in a 350°F oven for 30 minutes. Turn occasionally. Once the seeds have cooled, store in an airtight container.

❧ 363 ❧

Pumpkin Bread in a Jar
Baking quick breads in canning jars as a means of preservation was common during WWII. Here's a recipe for canned pumpkin bread.

⅔ c. shortening
2⅔ c. sugar
4 eggs
3⅓ c. flour
2 c. pumpkin
⅔ c. water
½ t. baking powder
2 t. baking soda
1½ t. salt
1 t. cinnamon
1 t. ground cloves
⅔ c. nuts, chopped (optional)

Cream the shortening and sugar. Beat in the eggs, pumpkin, and water. Sift the flour, baking powder, soda, salt, and spices. Add to the pumpkin mixture. Stir in the nuts. Pour into clean, greased, wide-mouth pint jars, filling them half full of batter. Bake in jars without lids at 325°F for about 45 minutes. The bread will rise and pull away from the sides of the jars. When done, remove one jar at a time from the oven, wipe the top clean, and screw a lid and band on firmly. Let cool on the counter away from drafts. A jar is sealed if the lid remains flat when pressed in the center. Shelf life is four to six months if stored in a cool, dry, dark place. If stored in the freezer, it can be kept one year.

From the kitchen of Nancy Feldman

From the Recipe Box

A recipe box filled with many favorite recipes gives us insight into a household and even different cultures of people. From examining a recipe box, we can often determine what foods are in plenty and common to that region, the foods favored, how simply the inhabitants of a particular region live, their lifestyle, and even their social ranking.

I suppose my recipe collection began when I was back in the sixth grade. The first time that I remember requesting a recipe from someone was when I was dining at my friend Cary's house. I can't recall what the main entrée was, but I sure did like the dressing on the garden salad. And so Mrs. Hill gave me her recipe. I brought it home, and it has been a part of our main recipe selection ever since.

When I first set up housekeeping on my own, I was about a six-hour drive from my hometown. Close friends teased me and asked if I was going to live off strawberry pies. I had just acquired Aunt Elsie's old 1950 Betty Crocker Picture Cookbook *and learned to bake fresh strawberry pies from scratch. Although I hadn't taken much interest in cooking as a child, I did know enough to keep us from starving. Well,* there I was, a new bride in a new town, nestled in St. Joe Beach on the Florida panhandle, and all alone during the day without transportation for the first few months. Was I ever lonely? During the day I would cross the road to the beach and stroll up and down the shore. Once I found live starfish washed ashore. Another time I found sand dollars. I spray-painted these and marked the year on them, strung a ribbon through one of the slits, and hung them as tree ornaments. Another day I discovered crabs and so began the chase. I managed to catch a few and brought them back to our tiny beach cottage for a taste of the gulf's offerings. We ate our fill of boiled shrimp quite often, too, as the Shrimp Shack just a few blocks away sold fresh shrimp for ninety-nine cents a pound. Never eat oysters in a month that doesn't have an R in it, I learned. It was in Port St. Joe that I tasted oyster stew for the first time. An immediate family favorite and a regional delicacy. That recipe was quickly added to my box for future dinner-table appearances. The panhandle is certainly a capital area for the freshest, best seafood ever, my favorite food. Apalachicola, East Point, and Carrabelle still hold secret Florida's best-kept seafood treasures. And I hope it remains that way.

Reflecting back two decades, I remember a retired couple from town who owned the trio of tiny beach cottages and lived in the two-story house just in front. Often they would invite me over in the early afternoon for a slice of pie and conversation. It was nice, and helped to ease my homesickness. I also remember when my first package arrived in the mail. It was filled with recipe cards, all handwritten and dated by both my mother and maternal grandmother. To hold and study the cards penned in their hands, now clasped lovingly in mine, and their treasured recipes was like coming home again to me.

More than twenty years ago, those two precious ladies in my life sat down together on my behalf and penned their reliable recipes. Yes indeed, my collection of recipes has grown and multiplied immensely since then. Now, I even concoct a few of my own. I have kept every one of those first recipe cards with me all this time and would never consider replacing them. They are a part of my treasured possessions. From them I know my mother's and grandmother's love. Love strengthens like silk cords, weaving together generational ties, passed on through hands that caress, stir, knead, roll, mix, blend, and transcribe from their recipe boxes to mine. Share your recipes—show your love.

❧ *364* ❧

Dish-Washing Gel (aka Jelly Soap)
Grate ½ lb. of bar soap into flakes and place in a large pot with ½ gal. of water. Stir to dissolve the flakes. Boil for 10 minutes, stirring frequently. Pour into a glass jar and allow to cool without a lid. Once cool, cover to prevent the soap from drying. As the soap sits, it will thicken to a gel consistency.

To use: Pour dish-washing gel into a squirt-top bottle until it's one-quarter or half full. Add hot water to the squirt bottle and shake before pouring into the sink. (Works best when dissolved under hot running water.)

❧ *365* ❧

Baking Powder Substitute
2 parts cream of tartar
1 part cornstarch
1 part baking soda
Mix the ingredients together and store in a labeled container. Measure out as you would ordinary baking powder.

❦ *366* ❦

Pumpkin Pie Spice
3 t. cinnamon
1 t. allspice
1 t. cloves
1 t. nutmeg
Combine and store in a labeled container.

❦ *367* ❦

Sweetened Condensed Milk
1 c. powdered milk
⅓ c. boiling water
⅔ c. sugar
3 T. butter
Mix in a blender for a couple of minutes until smooth.
Store the unused portion in the refrigerator.
   From the kitchen of Debbie Bohannon

❦ 368 ❦

Rice Milk (Milk Substitute)
Yield: 1 qt.
4 c. water
1 c. cooked brown rice
1 t. vanilla extract
Add ingredients to a blender and whip until smooth. Chill.

Note: For a smooth milk product, pour through a strainer. Or let sit until the sediment sinks to the bottom. Then pour into a jar, leaving the sediment in the bottom of the blender.

❦ 369 ❦

Make whipped cream with evaporated milk for use in ice cream or pudding and cake toppings. The key to success is to have the evaporated milk, the bowl, and the beater thoroughly chilled first. To whip, pour milk into the cold bowl, and whip with chilled beaters as for cream.

❧ *370* ❧

Buttermilk Made Easy
Add 1 T. buttermilk to a pint jar and fill with milk, or add 2 T. buttermilk to a quart jar and fill with milk. Screw on the lid and set in a warm place for 24 hours. Shake off and on throughout the process. Refrigerate when ready. Save back 1 or 2 T. to make another batch.
From the kitchen of Laine Amavizca

❧ *371* ❧

Homemade Butter
If you are blessed with a source for farm-fresh milk, you can make your own butter. Here are two methods.

By hand: Ladle the cream that has risen to the top of the milk jug into a glass jar and seal tightly. Do *not* fill the container more than half full. Now for the fun part. Shake, shake, shake, and then shake some more. Be inventive. Some people shake while rocking in a rocking chair. Try lining the children up on the sofa, giving each one a turn to shake ten times, then passing to the next one. Go around again and again. I've even heard of rolling the jar on the floor from one child to the next.

With a blender: Making butter in the blender frees up your hands for other projects. Ladle the fresh cream into the blender. You'll need a little of the milk in there, too, to help it blend properly. Turn the blender on whip and let it go. Depending on your blender, it takes about 10 minutes.

Notes on butter making, either method: There's no secret to making butter. It just requires a steady back-and-forth motion. However, if the cream gets too warm, it won't make butter; if it's too cold, it'll take longer. That's it. You'll know when it's ready; the butter will glob together in the jar. Remove the butter from the blender or jar with a large slotted spoon and place in a deep bowl. What you have left in the blender or jar is buttermilk. Use it to make buttermilk pancakes, bread, or biscuits. To finish the butter-making process, work the butter in the bowl by pressing with a large spoon. Press and pour off any liquid. Rinse the butter in the bowl under gently running water. Pour and press off the liquid again. This step is important because any buttermilk left in the butter will cause the butter to sour and yield an off taste sooner. Then stir in salt to taste and store in the freezer until needed, or refrigerate.

If milk cows are scarce in your neck of the woods, purchase whipping cream in the grocery store. Everyone needs to make butter at home at least once!

🐜 *372* 🐜

Honey-Butter

Honey-butter is expensive to purchase, yet simple to duplicate at home. Allow ¼ lb. of butter to soften slightly at room temperature. Place in a mixing bowl and add ¼ c. of honey. Blend together with a mixer. Add more honey, until you reach your desired sweetness. As a variation ⅛ t. ground cinnamon may be added. Pour the spread in attractive containers and store in the refrigerator. Honey-butter is perfect paired with warm dinner rolls.

❧ *373* ❧

Better-than-Margarine Spread

Here's a spread that reduces the fat and stretches the butter. It's also much healthier than margarine. Mix equal portions of butter and canola oil together until blended. Store the creamy spread in a tub in the refrigerator.

❧ *374* ❧

Butter Extender

Butter supply low? Here's a way to stretch butter.

One lb. butter plus 2 c. evaporated milk equal 2 lbs. butter. Try it and see. Let the butter come to room temperature, then beat it to cream using an egg beater or electric mixer. Add 2 c. evaporated milk, a little at a time. Keep beating until the milk is completely absorbed. Chill until firm, and you've doubled the butter supply.

※ *375* ※

Simple Beginner's Cheese *(Queso Blanco)*
Place 1 gal. of milk in a stainless-steel stockpot. Heat to 190°F, stirring several times. Remove from heat. Add ½ c. of vinegar or lemon juice and stir. Let rest for 10 minutes as curds form. Pour contents into a colander or strainer lined with cheesecloth or a muslin bag. Tie the bag or cloth and hang for 1 hour, allowing the whey to drain. Salt to taste and refrigerate or freeze.

Variation: To turn this into a hard cheese, immediately after pouring it into the colander, season with salt and place the cheese in cloth in a cheese press for a couple of hours with 10 lbs. of pressure.

From the kitchen of Bonnie Plasse

※ *376* ※

Making Yogurt at Home
Yogurt tastes great, but it's expensive, especially when you buy the flavored varieties. It's easy to prepare. A yogurt

machine is not required, but you will need a cooking thermometer.

Heat 1 qt. of milk in a pot on the stove to 180°F. Add 1 t. vanilla extract and allow milk to cool down to 110°F. (Set the pot in a larger pan of cool water to hurry the process.) Add 6 T. yogurt with live active cultures. (Any store-bought yogurt will work as long as it has aci-dophilus. Check the label.) Pour into a clean glass jar and screw on the lid. The jar must be maintained at 110°F undisturbed for the next 6 hours, which can be achieved several ways. Select a method from the following: Place in a gas oven without heat. Or use an electric heating blan-ket on low. Or heat water on the stove to 110°F, pour into an ice chest, and set the jar in the chest. Close the lid. It's that simple. Chill before serving.

From the kitchen of Deloris Massey

❧ *377* ❧

Homemade Granola

Now that you've got the yogurt, how about a spoonful of homemade granola to eat with it?

Yield: 4 qts. (recipe doubles easily)

In a Dutch oven or roasting pan mix 5 c. rolled oats, ½ c. wheat bran, ½ c. wheat germ, 1 c. chopped almonds or meal, 1 c. sunflower seeds, ½ c. powdered milk, 1 c. coconut flakes.

Warm ½ c. vegetable oil, 2 t. vanilla extract, and 1 c. honey, sorghum, or molasses together. Pour over the dry ingredients in the pan and stir through to combine. Bake at 250°F for 1 hour, stirring every 15 minutes. Remove from the oven and add 1½ c. dried fruit combination and stir.

Dried fruit suggestions: raisins, apples, papaya, mangoes, pineapples, dates. Enjoy at breakfast with milk or yogurt or spoon over ice cream for dessert.

Store in an airtight container.

❧ *378* ❧

Trail Mix Snack
A handy, healthy, and tasty treat made at a fraction of the cost.

To make, take a pint or as much as you wish of the homemade granola noted previously (tip #377) and add:
½ c. dried banana chips
½ c. peanuts or soy nuts
½ c. carob chips
½ c. yogurt-covered raisins.

❧ *379* ❧

Kettle Corn
Oil for popping
½ c. popcorn (unpopped)
3 T. sugar
Salt to taste

Heat oil in medium-size pot. Add the popcorn and sprinkle the sugar on top. Cover the pot with a lid and shake vigorously and continuously over the burner until the popping stops. Add salt to taste and serve immediately.
From the kitchen of Jim and Susan Erskine

❧ *380* ❧

Peanut Butter
If fresh raw peanuts are available, shell and pan-roast some on the stove in a large wok. After lightly roasting, grind the peanuts in a heavy-duty blender, grain mill, or juicer such as a Vitamix or a Champion juicer.

If fresh raw peanuts are not available, grind dry-roasted peanuts.

Add about 3 t. of pure raw honey to every 1 lb. of peanut butter and mix thoroughly. Store in the refrigerator.
From the kitchen of Brian Shilhavy

🦋 *381* 🦋

Frozen Yogurt
Easy to make. No ice cream churn or special equipment is needed.

Take plain yogurt (homemade or purchased) and add 1 cup of chopped fresh fruit or a can of fruit pie filling per every quart of yogurt, and stir to combine. Sweeten with sugar to taste and freeze in an airtight container. That's it!

🦋 *382* 🦋

Yogurt Cream Cheese
Line a colander with a thin cotton dish towel or muslin. Place the colander over a pan or bowl. Pour the yogurt into the colander and set it in the refrigerator overnight. Once the liquid has dripped down into the pan, the yogurt will be similar to, but slightly more tart in taste than, cream cheese.

❦ *383* ❦

Vinegar from Cider

Fill a gallon jar with fresh cider and cover with a kitchen towel or muslin cloth and rubber band. Label the jar, noting the starting date and scheduled removal date on the jar. Store in a warm dark spot without moving for 7 weeks. Return to the shelf if more time is needed. Strain before using to remove any film that may have formed on the surface.

❦ *384* ❦

Sauerkraut

Yield: 5 qts.

Shred 1 large head of cabbage. Place the shredded cabbage directly into sterilized canning jars. To each jar add 1 t. sugar and 1 t. pickling salt. Pour in enough ice-cold water to cover. Seal with a lid, but not tightly, to allow the fermentation process to take place. Store in a cool place (basement or root cellar) for 14 days.

From the kitchen of Ginger McNeil

❧ *385* ❧

Lemonade
The unique flavor in this recipe is brown sugar.
    To a 2 qt. pitcher add:
1 c. lemon juice, fresh squeezed or bottled
7 c. cool water
1½ c. light brown sugar
    Stir vigorously to blend and chill before serving.
    Serve with slices of lemon over ice.

❧ *386* ❧

Hot Spiced Apple Cider or Hot Spiced Tea
Into a Crock-Pot pour 1 pt. of Spiced Oranges (see tip #355) and at least 2 qts. of apple juice, apple cider, or black tea. Add cinnamon sticks for garnish and heat until warm. Stir well just before serving.

❧ 387 ❧

Sunny Summer Smoothie
Watermelon starting to soften? Don't throw it out. Make a
smoothie!
    Add the following to a blender and whip:
½ to 1 banana, peeled
1½ c. chopped watermelon (orange or yellow)
2 c. orange juice
1 T. honey
6 to 12 ice cubes
    Variation: Substitute pineapple juice for the orange
juice and honey.

❧ 388 ❧

Strawberry and Orange Juice Slush
Into a blender, add 2 c. frozen strawberries and 1½ c. orange juice, and blend. If using fresh berries, add 5 ice
cubes and 1½ c. orange juice and blend to combine. Serve
immediately.

❦ *389* ❦

Tiffany's Frozen-Fruit Smoothie
To the blender add 1 c. strawberries, 1 c. blueberries, and 1 banana, peeled and quartered. Add 1 c. orange juice and ½ c. grapefruit juice and blend. Serve immediately over crushed ice.

Recipe from Tiffany Tukua, our daughter, who created this beverage at the age of five.

❦ *390* ❦

Hot Lemon-Mint Tea
Add ½ t. lemon juice and a dash of crushed mint or lemon balm into a cup and pour in hot herbal tea. Allow to steep for several minutes. Sweeten to taste with honey, stevia, or raw sugar.

❦ *391* ❦

Growing Wheat Grass
In a seed starter tray, plant wheat berries just beneath the soil. (The same wheat you grind to make whole-wheat flour.) Water well. In a few days you should see growth. When the grass has grown up, cut about 1" off the top with scissors. The grass has a slightly sweet taste to it. The grass will continue to grow for a week or two. Clip some each day and juice. After the grass dies, reseed and start again. (See tip #338 for drying and 392 for juicing.)

❦ *392* ❦

Wheat Grass–Apple Juice Slush Drink
Add a handful of clippings of wheat grass to the blender with several ice cubes and fill with apple juice. Blend until the ice is chopped fine and the beverage is frothy! Drink immediately. This drink is extremely healthy and tastes great too!

🦋 *393* 🦋

Pastry Mix
Keep a supply of this pastry mix on hand for convenience
in pie making.
    To a container, add these dry ingredients:
4½ c. all-purpose flour
2 t. salt
Cut in 1½ c. shortening.
    To make one 9" pie shell: Remove 1½ c. of the mix and
add 2½ T. cold water. For a two-crust pie, use 3 c. mix and
approximately 5 T. water.

🦋 *394* 🦋

One-Pan Pie Pastry
Here's a no-mess piecrust, made in the pie pan!
Yield: 1 crust
1 c. whole-wheat pastry flour
¼ t. salt
¼ c. oil
3 T. water
    From The Oats, Peas, Beans & Barley Cookbook *by*
Edith Young Cottrell

Place the flour and salt in the pie pan. Measure the oil in a measuring cup and add the water. Beat with a fork until blended. Pour over the flour, stirring with a fork to mix evenly. Mix until well blended. Press into shape against the pan with your fingertips. Bake at 375°F for 20 minutes.

❧ 395 ❧

Grannie's Buttermilk Biscuits
2 c. sifted flour
½ t. baking soda
2 t. baking powder
1 t. sea salt
¼ c. shortening
1 c. cold buttermilk or sour milk
Mix the dry ingredients together, then cut in the shortening with two butter knives and stir in the buttermilk. Roll out the dough on a floured bread board and cut out biscuits. Bake on cookie tray at once in very hot oven, 450°F, for 12 minutes.

Variation: Mix in ½ c. grated cheese with the dry ingredients.

From the kitchen of Janie Jacobs, my deceased grannie

❧ 396 ❧

Mrs. Benham's Whole-Wheat Bread
Yield: 2 loaves
Mix 1 c. warm water, 2 packs dry yeast, and 1 T. honey
and set aside. In a separate bowl, mix 3 c. hot water, ¼ c.
honey, 4 T. oil, and 1½ T. salt. Let cool until lukewarm.
Then, add in 4½ c. flour. Add yeast mixture in the first
bowl to the second and let stand until double in bulk.
Add 4½ c. additional flour (9 c. total), or more if needed,
until the dough is stiff enough to handle. Knead for 8
minutes by hand. Divide the dough in half and place in
two lightly oiled loaf pans. Place in a 250°F oven for 15
minutes. Then set the oven to 350°F and bake for 30
more minutes until done.
From the kitchen of Hugh Godwin

❧ 397 ❧

Hush Puppies
Combine 1½ c. self-rising cornmeal, ½ c. flour, and a dash
of salt and pepper. To the bowl, add 1 egg, beaten, ½ c.

onion, finely diced, and enough milk to moisten through-out. Heat oil in a skillet until hot and test 1 t. of the batter in the hot oil to ensure that the batter will hold together. Make hush puppies into fritters (flatten with spatula) or shape into small balls in your hand before frying.

From the kitchen of Phyllis Lewis

❧ 398 ❧

Scandinavian Flat Bread
3 c. all-purpose flour
3 T. sugar
⅓ c. shortening
½ t. baking soda
½ t. salt
1 c. buttermilk
Mix the above ingredients. Roll the dough thin and brush with egg white. Sprinkle on caraway, sesame, and poppy seeds. Cut into 1" strips and bake at 350°F until brown and crispy.

From the kitchen of Chef Chuck Ferguson

⚜ *399* ⚜

Instant Corn-Bread Mix
    Mix together and place in a jar or Ziploc bag:
3 c. cornmeal
2 c. whole-wheat flour
6 t. baking powder
½ t. salt
1 c. sugar or ¾ c. honey
½ c. shortening
    When ready to bake, add 3 eggs plus 2½ c. milk. Stir until moistened. Put in a 9 × 13 pan. Bake at 425°F for 20 to 30 minutes.
    From the kitchen of Arlene Nyhoff

⚜ *400* ⚜

Homemade Honey Graham Crackers
Yield: About 6 dozen crackers
1 c. shortening

1 c. brown sugar
1 c. white sugar
1 c. honey
1 t. vanilla extract
4 c. wheat flour
2 c. white flour
½ t. salt
1 t. baking soda
2 t. baking powder
1 c. sweet milk

Cream shortening and sugars and honey until fluffy. Add vanilla. Sift the flour. Measure and add the salt, soda, and baking powder. Sift again. Add the sifted dry ingredients alternately with milk. Mix thoroughly after each addition. Chill the dough overnight. The next morning, turn it out on a floured board and roll as thin as possible. Cut in squares. Place 1" apart on a greased cookie sheet. Bake at 350°F until golden brown, approximately 10 to 15 minutes.

From the kitchen of Sylvia Britton

❧ *401* ❧

My Family's Favorite Omelets
Yield: Serves 4:
My mother claims these are the best omelets she's ever tasted. They're hearty and delicious.
4 hot, freshly baked small to medium potatoes, grated
1 onion, grated or chopped
½ c. ripe tomatoes, chopped
1 green tomato or bell pepper, chopped
¼ c. banana pepper rings or Pepperoncini, chopped (optional)
1 c. cooked meat of your choice: cubed ham, fried bulk sausage, or crumbled bacon
½ to ¾ c. cheddar cheese, grated
Garlic powder, salt, and pepper to taste
8 eggs, beaten with milk, salt, and pepper
Allow time to bake the potatoes just before making the omelets. Once the potatoes are done, slice them in half lengthwise. Allow to cool slightly to the touch, then grate warm potato halves into a bowl. (Discard the skins.) Add the chopped vegetables, meat, cheese, and seasonings into the bowl and stir to combine.

Pour enough egg mixture into a hot, lightly oiled skillet to make one omelet. Allow to cook on one side and then turn. Cover half of the omelet in the pan with a generous heap of filling, fold in half, and turn once. Remove and serve immediately. Continue until all four omelets are ready.

✸ 402 ✸

Muesli
A delicious breakfast cereal.
Mix the following into an airtight container and store in the refrigerator.
4 c. flaked oats
2 c. dried fruit combination
1 c. coconut flakes
1 c. almond or pecan meal
2 large apples, grated with the skins on
2 c. milk
½ c. honey
Stir to combine and chill before serving. Offer additional milk and honey for each individual bowl. Use within a week.

Variation for shelf storage: To store this cereal in the pantry for a longer period of time, make as above, omitting the fresh apples, milk, and honey. Add milk and honey to individual bowls with the cereal when ready to serve.

❧ 403 ❧

Sour Cream–Blueberry Pancakes

This recipe is great because you can use any basic pancake mix you have on hand; just reduce the amount of milk by ½ c. and replace with ½ c. sour cream instead. After the pancake mix has been thoroughly blended, add ¼ to ½ c. of blueberries, fresh or frozen. Prepare on a hot, lightly oiled griddle as usual.

❧ *404* ❧

Blueberry Syrup
Perfect on pancakes, cheesecake, ice cream, or yogurt.

Add 1 pt. of blueberries to a pot on the stove, along with a little water. Cook until the berries are tender, then mash. Stir in enough honey (½ c., more or less) to thicken to your desired consistency and ¼ c. of brown sugar. Store in the refrigerator.

❧ *405* ❧

Pancake/Waffle Syrup

2 c. water

1 c. raw sugar

1 t. maple, almond, or vanilla flavoring

Cook the water and sugar together on the stove until the mixture begins to thicken. Remove from the heat and stir in the flavoring. Refrigerate any unused portions.

From the kitchen of Sylvia Britton

❧ *406* ❧

Honey-Strawberry Syrup

Chop ¾ c. strawberries or desired fruit in the blender. Place in a small saucepan with ½ c. clover or wildflower honey. Simmer, stirring frequently, until the mixture and flavors are blended. Pour into a container and store in the refrigerator.

❦ *407* ❦

Pumpkin-Banana Pancakes
An autumn breakfast specialty. The banana adds a sweet flavorful note to the pumpkin.
Yield: 1 dozen 4" to 5" pancakes
Dry Ingredients:
1½ c. flour
1¾ t. baking powder
¾ t. cinnamon
½ t. baking soda
½ t. salt
⅛ t. ground ginger
2 T. brown sugar
Wet Ingredients:
1 T. oil
1¼ c. buttermilk
2 eggs, beaten
¼ c. pumpkin
½ c. mashed overripe banana

Thoroughly mix all of the dry ingredients. Then add the wet ingredients, which have been combined thoroughly, and mix until smooth. Fry the pancakes on a hot griddle or pan. Serve with maple syrup.

Adapted from the kitchen of Jonni McCoy. From her book, Miserly Moms.

Note: Jonni's recipe contained no banana. To omit the banana, increase the pumpkin to ¾ c.

⚜ *408* ⚜

Making Pancake Mix

If you like the convenience of ready-made mixes, combine all the dry ingredients from the previous recipe times four. Store in an airtight container. You'll have a head start on four batches.

When you want to make one batch of pancakes: Scoop out 1¾ c. of the dry mix. Add the wet ingredients in the same quantity as indicated in the recipe above and stir to combine. Fry on a hot griddle.

❧ *409* ❧

Breakfast Casserole
Yield: Serves 6 to 8
1 lb. bulk sausage, browned and drained
6 eggs, beaten
2 c. milk
6 slices bread, torn into small pieces
1 t. sea salt
1 t. Mrs. Dash or Spike seasoning (optional)
1 t. dry mustard
1 cup cheddar cheese, grated

Crumble the browned, drained sausage into a 9 × 12 casserole pan along with the remaining ingredients. Stir well to combine and bake at 350°F for 45 minutes.

From the kitchen of Sandra Jacobs, my aunt

⚛ *410* ⚛

Pineapple-Banana Crisp

Yield: 8 servings, 4 oz.each

3 to 4 medium bananas, sliced in coins

20 oz. can pineapple tidbits, drained (reserve ⅓ c. pineapple juice)

1½ t. cornstarch

1 c. bran or corn cereal flakes with raisins, crushed with a rolling pin

¼ c. flaked oats

¼ c. sunflower seeds

¼ c. firmly packed light brown sugar (optional)

⅓ c. flaked coconut

4 T. butter, melted

In a 1 qt. baking dish, place enough sliced bananas to cover the bottom. Add the drained pineapple. Mix the reserved pineapple juice and cornstarch and pour over the fruit.

In a small bowl, add the remaining ingredients and stir to moisten. Spoon the topping evenly over the fruit. Bake at 350°F for 20 minutes or until heated through.

❧ *411* ❧

Banana-Bread French Toast

Prepare your favorite banana-bread recipe at least a day ahead. (Bake in a loaf pan to slice like bread.) Beat 2 eggs or more and place in a pie pan. Add about ½ c. milk and stir to blend. Slice the banana bread into ½" to ¾" slices. Fry each slice in a lightly oiled pan after dipping and coating each side in the egg and milk mixture. Turn once. Top each serving with the syrup of your choice. Serve with fried sausage and fresh apple slices on the side.

❧ *412* ❧

Chicken and Apple Toast

This recipe is prepared much like chicken salad. Boil a chicken, parts, or use leftover baked chicken or turkey. Separate the meat from the bones and cut into bite-size pieces or shred. Discard the bones. (One chicken breast will yield enough spread for 2 slices of toast.) Add the following ingredients to the cooked chicken in the quantity you prefer. In a bowl add chopped meat, chopped fresh apple, a little minced onion, finely chopped celery (optional), and a sprinkle of sea salt, Mrs. Dash, or Spike seasoning. Add mayonnaise 1 T. at a time until the mixture is moistened to your liking.

Spread 2 to 3 T. of the mixture onto a slice of bread. Place the bread with its topping under a broiler until the spread is hot and the bread crusts appear to toast. (Store leftover mixture in the refrigerator up to four days.)

From the kitchen of Delores Stafford, my mother

🐦 *413* 🐦

Columbia Salad Dressing
1 c. mayonnaise
¼ c. ketchup
1 T. soy sauce
¼ t. garlic powder
1 t. lemon juice or ½ fresh lemon
1 T. water
½ t. paprika (optional)

Thoroughly blend all ingredients and store in the refrigerator.

From the kitchen of Mrs. Frank Hill

❦ *414* ❦

French Dressing
⅓ t. sea salt
¼ t. paprika or pepper
1 t. mustard
4 T. olive oil
1½ T. vinegar of your choice
    Blend the salt, paprika or pepper, and mustard in a small bowl. Pour in the oil and stir well to blend. Add the vinegar, beating with a fork.
    Serving suggestion: Use with Tomato and Lima Bean Salad. See tip #431.
    From the kitchen of Marilouise Wilkerson

❦ *415* ❦

Sweet-and-Sour Sauce (for meat balls or little smokies sausages)
This sauce is a caterer's treasured secret.
48 oz. Concord grape jelly
20 oz. (or more to taste) barbecue sauce of your choice

Heat in a pot and stir to blend thoroughly. Add meat balls or little smokies sausages to the warm sauce and heat through. A Crock-Pot works great for this recipe.

See tip #417 for Honey Barbecue Sauce.

From the kitchens of Delores Stafford and Deborah Tukua

🐉 *416* 🐉

Steak Sauce
2 c. ketchup
2 garlic cloves, minced
⅔ c. chopped onion
½ c. lemon juice
½ c. water
½ c. Worcestershire sauce
½ c. vinegar
¼ c. soy sauce
¼ c. packed dark brown sugar
2 T. prepared mustard

Combine the ingredients in a saucepan and bring to a boil. Reduce the heat to low and simmer for 30 minutes. Pour into bottle(s) and allow to cool. Once cool, cap and store in the refrigerator.

From the kitchen of Jonni McCoy. Excerpted from her book, Miserly Moms.

🦋 *417* 🦋

Honey Barbecue Sauce
Yield: 3 pts.
4 c. tomato puree (process fresh tomatoes in a blender)
1 t. minced garlic
4 T. brown sugar
½ c. honey
½ t. cumin
2 T. Mrs. Dash
4 T. prepared mustard
8 t. flour
1 c. apple cider vinegar
1½ to 2 t. Worcestershire sauce
1 T. sea salt
3 t. turmeric
2 t. ground dry mustard
1 t. Liquid Smoke

Mix all the ingredients together in a large pot on the stove and heat to boiling. Turn down the heat and allow to simmer for 5 more minutes. Pour immediately into hot, sterilized jars. Allow to cool to room temperature, then refrigerate or freeze. (See tip #355 for water-bath canning instructions.)

❧ *418* ❧

Treasure Chip Cookies
Yield: 3 dozen cookies
½ c. butter, softened
1½ c. raw sugar (or light brown sugar)
1 egg
1 t. vanilla extract
1½ c. all-purpose flour (or whole-wheat pastry flour)
1½ t. baking powder
¼ t. salt
1 c. raisins (use ½ c. golden and ½ c. dark)
½ c. sunflower seeds
½ c. carob chips

Combine the butter, sugar, egg, and vanilla and beat until light. Add the dry ingredients and mix to combine. Stir in the raisins, sunflower seeds, and carob chips. Drop by the tablespoon onto greased cookie sheets. Bake on the top rack of the oven for approximately 10 minutes at 350°F. Remove the cookies and cool on a wire rack.

✵ *419* ✵

Maple Bread Pudding
7 slices bread
3 c. scalded milk
⅔ c. maple syrup
2 eggs, beaten
1 t. salt
1 t. cinnamon
½ c. raisins

Break the bread into pieces and place in a buttered baking dish. Pour the scalded milk over it. Stir in the remaining ingredients, which have been mixed together, and bake 1 hour at 350°F. Serve hot with cream, milk, or whipped cream.

From the kitchen of Cathy Toppen

❧ *420* ❧

Maple Syrup Pecan Pie
Yield: 1 9" pie
2 c. maple syrup
4 eggs
⅓ t. salt
1 c. chopped or halved pecans
   Beat together the first three ingredients. Pour into an unbaked 9" pie shell. Top with the chopped nuts. Bake at 375°F for approximately 30 minutes.
   From the kitchen of Cathy Toppen

❧ *421* ❧

Pumpkin-Pear Pie
Yield: 1 9" pie
Pear adds a gourmet flavor to traditional pumpkin pie. To make pear sauce, see the following recipe.
¾ c. canned pumpkin
¾ c. pear sauce (or applesauce)
½ c. brown sugar

½ c. raw sugar

1 t. ginger

¼ t. cloves

½ t. cinnamon

2 eggs

1 c. milk, scalded

Combine the first two ingredients; add the sugar and spices. Beat in the eggs and milk. Pour into a 9" pie shell and bake at 375°F for 60 minutes.

Adapted from the kitchen of Susan Dahlem

Note: Susan's recipe uses applesauce. Try either fruit sauce.

🧩 422 🧩

Homemade Pear or Apple Sauce

Core and peel pears or apples and chop. (Save the peelings to make jelly. See tip #423.) Place in an open pot with water and let cook until soft. If you like texture and chunky sauce, hand-mash. If a smoother variety is preferred, insert an electric hand mixer into the pot of cooked fruit and whip. (The sauce can be enjoyed fresh, frozen, or home canned.)

Note: If you have a pear tree with hard cooking pears on it, soften the meat and remove the skin at the same time by placing whole fruit in the pressure cooker or canner with some water for about 10 minutes, depending on the hardness of the pears. Remove the peels, cores, and stems and transfer the pears to a pot on the stove to cook as instructed above.

423

Apple Jelly from Peelings

Take the apple peelings left after making applesauce and place in a large saucepan. (There should be at least 3 qts.) Discard all stems and blossom ends and any imperfect, blemished peelings. Add 4 to 5 c. of water to the apple skins. Cover the pan and allow to simmer until the skins are soft and the juice from the skins has colored and flavored the water (at least 1 hour). Strain the juice from the peels and measure out as many cups of the juice as your jelly recipe calls for.

❧ *424* ❧

Fresh Apple Cake
1 c. raw sugar
1 c. brown sugar
3 c. all-purpose or whole-wheat pastry flour
1½ c. vegetable oil
3 c. fresh apple chunks or slices
2 eggs, beaten
1 c. nuts, chopped
1 c. raisins
1 t. baking soda
1 t. sea salt
1 t. ground cinnamon
1 t. vanilla extract

Mix all the ingredients in a casserole pan. The batter will be stiff. Bake for approximately 75 minutes at 275°F.

Variation: In place of the 1 c. nuts, try ½ c. sunflower seeds and ½ c. pecan meal.

From the kitchen of Ann Kay

❧ *425* ❧

Lemon Pudding
Tasty hot or chilled.
Yield: 7 servings, ½ c. each
Mix 1½ c. sugar and ⅓ c. plus 1 T. cornstarch well. Gradually stir in 1½ c. water. Cook over medium heat to a boil. Cook about 1 minute. Quickly stir in 2 egg yolks. (Crack the egg yolks and place in a small bowl ahead of time.) Boil 1 minute and remove from the heat. While hot, add 3 T. butter, 2 t. grated lemon rind, and ½ c. lemon juice. Continue to stir until the ingredients are blended well and the butter has dissolved.

Recipe doubles and triples easily.
From the kitchen of Marilyn Leland

❧ *426* ❧

Growing Green Salad Sprouts
In a wide-mouth ½-gallon jar, add 3 to 4 T. of a variety of sprouting seeds: alfalfa, red clover, fenugreek, bean seeds, etc. Fill the jar one-third full of water; set up overnight. In

the morning, drain off the water through a screen lid or im-provise. Rinse with clean water and drain again. Out of di-rect sunlight, set the jar at an angle to allow the seeds ade-quate drainage. When the seeds show signs of growth, usually white sprouts, place near a window. Continue to rinse the sprouts twice daily and set them at an angle to al-low drainage, or the sprouts will sour. The sprouts should mature in three to four days. Remove and add to your fa-vorite salad or refrigerate.

🦅 *427* 🦅

Chickweed–Bean Sprouts Salad
A delicious winter salad.

Combine equal amounts of freshly picked chickweed and bean/green sprouts. (See tip #428 for growing sprouts.) Top with your favorite dressing and enjoy. (Chickweed can be found in the wild or growing in your lawn in winter. Rich in vitamin C. Don't pick from chemi-cally sprayed lawns, though.)

❦ 428 ❦

Sicilian Tomato Salad

Slice tomatoes into wedges. Slice red onions very thin. (A good ratio is two-thirds tomato to one-third onion.) Combine the two and sprinkle with oregano and salt to taste. Drizzle with olive oil. Toss, chill, and serve.

From the kitchen of Jane Fenner

❦ 429 ❦

Tomato and Lima Bean Salad

4 large tomatoes

1½ c. cooked baby lima beans or butter beans

1 very small onion, grated

1 T. chopped parsley

½ c. nuts, finely chopped, or pecan meal

2 T. celery, minced, or a dash of celery salt

Salt and pepper to taste

French Dressing (see tip #414)

Cut a slice from the top of each tomato. Using a teaspoon, remove the pulp. To the cooked beans, add the onion, parsley, chopped nuts or nut meal, celery, and seasonings. Mix a little French Dressing in and fill the tomatoes with the mixture. Pour more dressing over the top and serve.

From the kitchen of Marilouise Wilkerson

🌃 *430* 🌃

Broiled Green Tomatoes
Green tomatoes
Topping:
2 scallions
¾ c. feta or Parmesan cheese, grated
4 T. mayonnaise

To make the topping, chop the whole scallions into a small bowl. Grate feta or Parmesan cheese into the bowl (or use a shaker of Parmesan cheese) and stir in the mayonnaise. Slice the tomatoes—not too thin, so they remain firm—and drop 1 t. of topping onto the center of each slice of tomato. Place on a tray under the broiler for just a few minutes, until the topping begins to turn golden. Serve warm.

Note: Firm, ripe tomatoes can be used in place of green tomatoes, if preferred. Store unused topping in the refrigerator.

From the kitchen of Delores Stafford

❧ *431* ❧

Carrot-Raisin-Pineapple Salad

Grate 2 lbs. of fresh carrots. Drain one 20 oz. can of crushed pineapple and add a scoop of raisins. Mix all together with ¼ to ½ c. of mayonnaise and chill before serving.

❧ *432* ❧

Cottage Fries

Enjoy cottage fries without the grease of frying!

Scrub and slice potatoes in thin strips or wedges with the skins on and season with salt or Cajun seasoning. Lightly oil a cookie sheet and lay the potato fries on it. Bake at 400°F for about 25 minutes, until almost done. Then place the tray under the broiler until the fries are tender and golden. Turn at least once to brown both sides and make crispy.

🦋 *433* 🦋

Deborah's French Onion–Potato Soup
Yield: 6 servings, 8 oz. each
Sauté 1 onion, grated, in the bottom of a 2-qt. pot with ¼ c. butter until tender. To the same pot add:
4 c. water
4 to 5 medium potatoes, grated
2 t. dry beef bouillon
2 T. dry onion soup mix
1 t. sea salt
1 t. Worcestershire sauce

Simmer until the potatoes are tender and the soup thickens. Ladle into individual serving bowls. Top with garlic bread chips or garlic toast. Sprinkle grated mozzarella or extra-sharp cheddar cheese on top of the bread and heat in the oven or microwave until the cheese melts. Serve immediately.

❦ *434* ❧

Homemade Soup Stock or Beef Broth
Ask the local butcher for soup bones. If you can, select those with a little meat left on the bone for optimum
flavoring. The cost is minimal, but the flavor is maxi-
mum. Simmer the bones covered with water, vegetables—
especially onion—garlic, salt, and other desired spices for
at least 1 hour. Strain out and discard the vegetables after
the simmering process. This stock freezes or pressure-
cans well.

❦ *435* ❧

Home-Style Cream of _____ Soup
Here's a way to make your own healthy creamed soups,
eliminating MSG from your diet and an item from your
grocery list!
Melt 1 T. butter over low heat and stir in 1 T. flour.
Cook until the mixture begins to bubble. Remove from
the heat and stir in 1 c. milk. Return to low heat, stirring

constantly until thick. Add 1 t. salt or 1 t. dried chicken seasoning. Stir to dissolve. Add any of the following vegetables for the soup of your choice.

For Cream of Mushroom Soup, add ½ c. cooked chopped mushrooms.

For Cream of Celery Soup, add ¼ c. cooked diced celery.

For Cream of Broccoli Soup, add ½ lb. fresh, cooked broccoli, chopped, ¼ c. onions, chopped, and ¼ c. celery, diced and cooked. (Cook all vegetables together in water until tender.)

🐜 436 🐜

Crock-Pot Vegetable Cheese Chowder
Yield: 12 servings, 8 oz. each
3 c. chicken broth
1 c. potatoes, chopped
½ c. carrots, diced or shredded
½ c. celery, diced
½ c. onion, diced or grated
½ c. bell pepper, chopped
¼ c. butter

2 c. milk
Dash of pepper and garlic powder
1½ c. mozzarella cheese
1½ c. cheddar cheese
½ c. flour or instant potato flakes to thicken

Add all to a Crock-Pot and stir. Simmer until the potatoes are done. Stir several times during cooking.

Author's note: Cheddar cheese has a tendency to get lumpy in this soup recipe. That is why I've used two types of cheese. To increase the yield, add more water and cubed potatoes.

Adapted from the kitchen of Annette Godwin

🐦 437 🐦

Deborah's Pasta Salad
Yield: Serves 8 to 10
Bring ½ lb. ridged elbow macaroni and ½ lb. twist macaroni to a boil until tender. Drain and place in a large bowl.

To the cooked pasta, add:
1 bell pepper, chopped

7 oz. jar Spanish salad olives with pimiento strips, drained

6 oz. jar marinated artichoke hearts, chopped, with marinade

3 to 4 medium to large tomatoes, chopped

2 T. Spike seasoning

1 medium onion, diced

Cucumbers, broccoli, shredded carrots, or other raw vegetables (optional)

Toss the salad well. To make the dressing, combine the following and stir to blend:

½ c. red wine vinegar

1 c. salad oil

⅓ c. ketchup

½ c. honey or raw sugar

Dash of salt

Pour the sauce onto the pasta and stir to combine. Chill several hours before serving.

Variation: Add peeled, boiled shrimp. (When adding shrimp, the pasta will not keep fresh as long in the refrigerator.)

❦ *438* ❦

Romaine-Cabbage Salad with Honey Mustard Dressing
Yield: 6 servings
Dressing Ingredients:
½ c. mayonnaise
½ c. commercial sour cream
2 T. honey
1½ T. spicy brown mustard
⅓ c. pecan meal
Salad Ingredients:
3 c. shredded cabbage (use 1½ c. regular cabbage and
    1½ c. red cabbage for color)
2 c. shredded romaine lettuce
¼ c. thinly sliced red onion strips

Combine and chill the dressing ingredients. Cut the cabbage into long, coarse shreds. This is done by holding a quarter head of cabbage firmly against the cutting board. Use a chef's knife to slice it into shreds. To prepare the romaine, stack the leaves and slice with a chef's knife crosswise into long shreds.

To serve: Toss the salad greens, onions, and dressing mixture to coat. Serve immediately.

❦ *439* ❦

Fresh Broccoli and Bacon Salad

Chop 1 fresh head of broccoli and ½ head of cauli-flower. Add ½ c. of golden raisins and ¼ to ½ c. of fried bacon, crumbled, and stir. Blend 1 c. mayonnaise with 2 T. raw sugar and 2 T. vinegar. Pour the dressing over the produce and stir to coat.

From the kitchen of Delores Stafford

❦ *440* ❦

Corn on the Cob with Herbed Butter
Yield: 8 servings

Add ½ c. softened butter, ½ t. salt, 1 t. chives, 1 t. basil, and 1 t. oregano to a bowl and blend. Being careful not to remove them, pull back the husks of 8 ears of corn. Do remove the corn silk. Spread 1 T. of the herb butter on each ear of corn. Pull the husks back up over the corn to cover. Tightly wrap each ear of corn in a sheet of foil and bake at 375°F for about 30 minutes, or until the corn is tender.

❧ *441* ❧

Fried Dandelion Blossoms

Gather fresh dandelion blossoms in spring. Remove all stems, as they are very bitter to the taste. Wash and dry the dandelion blossoms on paper towels or a kitchen towel. Beat 1 egg well. Take a handful of blossoms at a time, coat in beaten egg, and remove with a slotted spoon. Add dandelions to a small paper sack containing dry bread crumbs or cracker crumbs. Hold it closed with your hand and shake to coat. Fry in hot cooking oil until golden brown, remove with a slotted spoon, drain on paper towels, and salt to taste.

From the kitchen of Sylvia Britton

❧ *442* ❧

Mexican Beans and Rice
This is a nice side dish accompaniment or quick-to-fix lunch.

Cook 1 c. of brown rice or open a jar of home-canned rice. (See tip #348.) Heat 1 qt. of chili bean mix (see tip

#344) in a pot. Spoon rice onto plates and top with chili beans and banana pepper rings, if desired. Great with Mexican corn bread.

443

Refried Beans

No need to purchase cans of refried beans again with Deborah's chili beans on hand. (See tip #342.) Open a jar of the prepared chili beans and mash with a fork. The chili beans convert into refried beans in a matter of minutes. Use in dips, tacos, or nachos! Yummy!

444

Poor Man's Lobster

Lightly brush the bottom of an oblong glass ovenware pan with melted butter or olive oil. Place codfish fillets in the pan and brush the top of each fillet with melted butter. Salt and pepper lightly to taste. Bake uncovered until tender at 325°F. When the meat separates easily with a fork, it's done.

Small cups of clarified butter should be offered with each individual place setting for dipping the fish, like lobster.

From the kitchen of Lowell Tukua

🦅 *445* 🦅

Linguine with White Clam and Artichoke Sauce
1 lb. linguine
6 oz. jar marinated artichoke hearts
4 T. butter
1 large clove garlic, chopped
2 T. flour
13 oz. can minced clams, liquid drained and reserved
2 medium carrots, shredded
4 T. chopped parsley
¾ t. dried thyme
¾ t. dried basil
Salt and pepper to taste

Cook the linguine according to the directions on the
package.

Drain the artichoke hearts, reserving the liquid; chop
into bite-size chunks. Heat the butter and garlic together in
a skillet for about 1 minute. Stir in the flour, reserved arti-

choke marinade, and reserved clam juice. Bring to a full boil, stirring continuously. Add the clams, artichoke hearts, carrots, parsley, thyme, and basil. Simmer for 5 minutes, stirring. Season to taste with sea salt and pepper. Serve over the hot cooked and drained linguine.

🦋 446 🦋

Plank-Baked Fresh Whole Fish

Here's an eye-appealing country way to serve whole fish—planking.

Select oak, hickory, or ash wood planks at least 1½" thick and long enough and wide enough to contain a whole fresh fish. Grease the plank and heat in the oven. Place a whole fish on the hot plank and season with salt and pepper. Brush on melted butter. Bake for 10 minutes per pound at 400°F. When the fish is about done, arrange hot mashed potatoes (sweet potatoes or Idaho potatoes) to one side of the fish (pipe with a cookie press for a gourmet presentation) and place under the broiler briefly to brown. Remove from the oven and serve individually on planks with piping hot vegetables such as broccoli or brussels sprouts positioned opposite the potatoes.

Adapted from Betty Crocker's Picture Cookbook *(1950 edition)*

❧ *447* ❧

Baked Maple Chicken
Yield: Serves 4 to 6
1 chicken (2½ to 3 lbs.), cut in pieces
¼ c. butter, melted
¼ c. maple syrup
½ t. lemon rind, grated
1 t. salt
Dash of pepper
¼ c. almonds, chopped
2 t. lemon juice

Place the chicken pieces in a shallow, buttered baking dish. Mix the remaining ingredients and pour evenly over the chicken. Bake uncovered 50 to 60 minutes at 325°F, basting occasionally. Especially good served with rice.

From the kitchen of Cathy Toppen

❦ *448* ❦

Good and Easy Pizza
Yield: 1 large pizza
1 pkg. dry yeast
1 T. honey
1¼ t. salt
2 T. olive oil
2½ c. whole-wheat flour
½ c. onion, diced
⅛ t. garlic powder
8 oz. tomato sauce
⅛ t. pepper
2 t. oregano flakes
14 oz. pepperoni slices (optional)
1 c. bulk sausage, cooked and drained
½ c. black olives
¼ c. bell peppers and mushrooms
2 c. mozzarella cheese, grated

Dissolve the yeast in 1 c. warm water. Stir in the honey, salt, oil, and flour. Beat vigorously twenty strokes. Shape the dough in an oiled pizza pan and bake 5 minutes at 425°F. Remove from the oven. Spread the tomato sauce mixed with spices on top of the crust. Add the remaining toppings, cheese last. Bake at 425°F for 20 to 25 minutes.

From the kitchen of Bonnie Plasse

❧ *449* ❧

Sausage-Squash Casserole
Yield: Serves 6
This serves well as a main entrée or a substitute for dressing with roast turkey or baked chicken.
1 lb. bulk sausage
1 clove garlic, minced
¼ c. onion, diced
½ c. milk
2 eggs, beaten
½ t. salt
Dash of pepper (optional)
1 T. dried parsley flakes
½ t. dried oregano flakes
½ c. grated Parmesan cheese
½ c. bread crumbs, dry or fresh
2 qts. home-canned yellow crookneck squash, drained
    (or 1½ qts. fresh-cooked squash)

Brown the bulk sausage in a skillet with the minced garlic and onion. Add the milk, eggs, salt, and spices to a 2 qt. casserole dish and beat with a fork. Add the cooked sausage, cooked squash, and remaining ingredients to the casserole dish and stir to combine. Bake at 325°F for 30 minutes.

❧ *450* ❧

Blender Quiche Recipes

On a farm, fresh eggs and milk are generally in abundance. Here are two of my recipes utilizing the basics in a contemporary fashion. With the use of the blender, making quiche is a breeze. Hope you enjoy these blender quiche recipes as much as our family does. (See tip #394 for One-Pan Pie Pastry recipe.)

Spinach Sausage Quiche

Fry ½ lb. bulk sausage and drain.

To a blender, add and mix:

3 eggs

1 c. milk

1 T. parsley flakes

1 T. flour of your choice

¾ t. salt

¼ t. garlic powder

½ t. onion powder or ¼ c. chopped onion

To a piecrust, add:

8 oz. drained spinach (or kale)

Cooked and drained bulk sausage

½ c. grated sharp cheddar or mozzarella cheese

Pour in the liquid mixture and bake at 375°F until the center is done, about 30 minutes. (Test with a knife.)

❧ *451* ❧

Crab Quiche

To a blender, add and mix:

1 c. milk

1 T. flour

3 eggs

½ t. salt

1 t. thyme

½ t. onion powder or ¼ c. chopped onion

In a piecrust, place:

1 can crabmeat, drained

1 small pkg. cream cheese, chunked

Handful of Spanish olives and pimientos, halved

Pour in the liquid mixture from the blender and bake in a 375°F oven until the center is set, approximately 30 minutes.

Variations: Salad-size boiled and peeled shrimp can be used in place of the crabmeat. Or try a can of drained tuna. Make good use of leftover baked fish, especially cod, flounder, or catfish, by crumbling up in the pie in place of crabmeat.

❧ *452* ❧

Creamy Crock-Pot Roast (Crock-Pot Recipe)
4 lb. venison or beef roast
1 envelope dry onion soup mix
½ to 1 c. milk
1 small onion, chopped
¼ c. red wine vinegar
1 large carrot, grated

Combine everything except the meat in the Crock-Pot. Stir to blend ingredients. Cut the roast in half, if necessary, to fit in the Crock-Pot and cover. Simmer on low overnight or equivalent hours. Thicken gravy with cornstarch or flour, if desired, before serving. Serve over a bed of rice or mashed potatoes.

🐲 *453* 🐲

Fried Venison Steak
2 to 3 lbs. venison steaks (or chops)
Buttermilk
Salt and pepper and garlic powder to taste
1 onion, chopped
Flour
Cooking oil
Marinate the steaks in buttermilk at least 1 hour before frying. Season both sides of the steaks with salt, pepper, and garlic powder. Dust the steaks with flour and brown on both sides in a hot skillet with cooking oil. (Add just enough oil to cover the bottom of the skillet.) Remove the steaks from the skillet, drain on paper towels, and prepare the gravy.

To make gravy: Stir 2 T. flour into the hot pan drippings. Brown the flour then, while being sure to keep the skillet hot, slowly stir in 1 c. of water. Allow the mixture to become hot again and stir in another cup of water. Add 1 chopped onion; season to taste with salt, pepper, and garlic powder. The gravy will thicken as it continues to cook. Return the steaks to the gravy, cover, and simmer on low until the steaks are tender. Stir occasionally.

Serving suggestion: Serve over rice or mashed potatoes. Venison chops can be prepared using this same method.

From the kitchen of Delores Stafford

❦ *454* ❦

Quick-and-Easy Chili
Yield: 5 qts.
This recipe utilizes the quart jars of chili beans from tip #343.

Fry 1 to 1½ lbs. ground beef, turkey, or venison. Drain off the grease and place in a pot. To the pot, add the contents of two quart jars of chili beans, 1 qt. canned, quartered tomatoes, and 1 pt. tomato sauce. Stir to combine, heat through, and serve.

ꕥ *455* ꕥ

Enchilada Tower
Yiels: 6 servings
1 lb. ground beef, turkey or venison
Salt and pepper to taste
1 qt. home-canned chili beans (see tip #343)
1 pt. chopped tomatoes (drain if using canned)
Flour tortillas, large
1½ c. shredded sharp cheddar cheese
Banana pepper rings, black olives, diced or green chilis
    (optional)

Brown the ground beef in a deep skillet and season to taste with salt and pepper. Drain. Add a jar of Deborah's chili beans and the chopped tomatoes. Stir to combine and heat.

In a 4½ qt. Dutch oven, place a layer of the meat and bean mixture, the size of a tortilla, in the bottom of the pot. Top with a flour tortilla and a handful of shredded cheese. Sprinkle on diced olives, green chilis, or banana pepper rings, if desired. Repeat the layering process until the meat-bean mix has all been used or the tower is near the top of the pot. End with cheese and pepper rings on top. Cover with a lid and place in a preheated 325°F oven until the cheese melts and the tortillas soften, approximately 25 minutes.

To serve: Cut through the Enchilada Tower from the top center through all the layers, like slicing a layer cake or pie. Top servings with picante sauce and/or sour cream, if desired.

Variation: Add a pint of black beans to the beef and bean mixture.

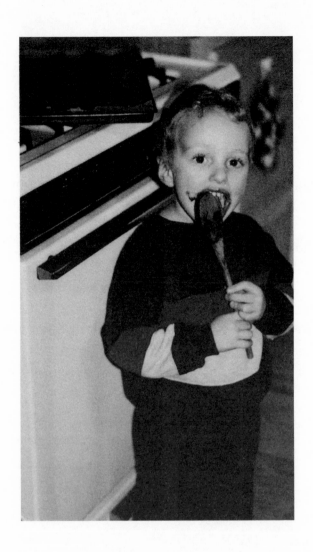

Children's Cooking
(Recipes for Beginning Cooks)

As children show an interest in cooking, their assistance should be welcomed in the kitchen. There are many things that little ones can do to participate. Our three-and-a-half-year-old sets the table, stirs the tuna salad, helps drop the chocolate candy batter onto the tray, then licks the spoon or pot clean. The yummiest job of all! The more familiar children are with cooking, the more comfortable they will be in the kitchen as adults. Everyone eats, so everyone needs to know how to feed himself and others. With all the pressures of studies or marriage or launching a new career that await them, it would be nice to know that by the time our children venture out into the world, they are well equipped to take care of their needs successfully.

Children love having their very own cookbook. As my children were growing up, I bought cookbooks especially for them to use and learn from. When trying a new recipe for the first time, we wrote the date at the top of the page and the family members that participated in the preparations. It is amazing how fast time flies and how quickly children grow, and now it's fun to look back and remember those first cooking sessions. The following section is specifically designed in the hopes of sparking an interest in cooking among children of all ages. The recipes are given in order of difficulty with the easiest to prepare shown first. Included are recipes that my children learned to make at home in our kitchen. What better way to make fond memories with our blessings than to prepare a meal or snack with them, then partake of it together afterwards. With our encouragement, cooking can also be a wonderful way to build their confidence. Whether you select a lunch a week or a dessert a week or an entire Sunday dinner for your children to accomplish, I encourage you to set aside a regular weekly slot for fun cooking with your kids. You'll all be glad you did. After you master these recipes, search out the main recipe section of this book. I am sure there are many things that you and your family will be able to prepare together once you've learned the basics of cooking. Don't forget to write the date next to the recipe the first time you prepare it. List everyone's name that participated and rate how your family liked the dish as well.

❧ *456* ❧

Ants on a Log
Wash stalks of celery, cut off the ends and half each stalk.
Spread peanut butter in the well of each section of celery
and top with dark raisins.

❧ *457* ❧

Root Beer Float
Put one or two scoops of vanilla ice cream into a tall glass.
Slowly pour in some root beer or birch beer, making sure
that it doesn't overflow. Serve with a spoon and a straw.

🦋 458 🦋

Peanut Butter–Honey Toast
Toast as many slices of bread as you need to serve. Spread peanut butter on the top of each. Drizzle honey on top of the peanut butter and serve immediately while hot.

🦋 459 🦋

No-Cook Peanut Butter Fudge
Mix these ingredients in a bowl:
1 cup peanut butter, crunchy or smooth
1 cup light corn syrup (Karo syrup)
1¼ c. confectionery powder sugar, sifted
1¼ c. nonfat dry powdered milk
Add more powdered milk, up to 1½ c. if needed to thicken more. Use a spoon to mix these ingredients until the batter is too stiff to stir. Then finish combining thoroughly with your hands. Spread the mixture into a 9-inch square pan and cut into fudge bars to serve.

※ *460* ※

Banana Boats
You'll need one ripe banana per person.
Take each banana, leaving the skins on, and cut about halfway through lengthwise. Pull the peels back slightly and fill the cavity with carob or chocolate chips, peanut butter or peanuts and miniature marshmallows. Here are three different ways to cook. Select your preference.

Method 1: Put the skin back into place and set on a tray. Warm in the oven until the chocolate chips and marshmallows melt and the banana softens.

Method 2: Warm in the microwave until the chocolate melts.

Method 3: To grill outdoors, center each stuffed banana on a sheet of aluminum foil and wrap tightly. Place on the grill over hot coals for approximately 7 minutes. Remove from the foil and eat with a spoon. The banana should be soft and easy to spoon out.

461

Cheese Toast
Toast as many slices of bread as you need to serve. Place the toast on a baking sheet and top each with a slice of your favorite cheese. Place the try directly under the hot broiler. Broil until the cheese starts to melt and turns golden. Cheese broils quickly, so check after a couple of minutes. Serve immediately, while hot. Serve with a fruit cup for a complete breakfast. See recipe below.

462

Apple-Raisin Salad (Waldorf Salad)
I've substituted yogurt for mayonnaise for a flavor you'll enjoy, and raisins for nuts to economize.
2 to 3 red apples
1 c. raisins
1 stalk of celery, diced
¼ c. grated coconut
3 T. vanilla yogurt
Wash then chop the apples into bite-size chunks, leaving the skins on for color. Place in a serving bowl with the

raisins, diced celery, and grated coconut. Fold in 3 T. vanilla yogurt until all is thoroughly combined. Serve at once or chill.

❧ 463 ❧

Tuna Salad Sandwiches
Yield: 5 or 6 sandwiches
2 6 oz. cans of tuna in spring water
3 T. pecan meal
1 t. granulated garlic
4 T. mayonnaise
2 T. onion, diced
¼ to ½ c. fresh tomato, chopped
1 egg, hardboiled (optional)
Combine the above ingredients in a mixing bowl and spread on bread. Top with another slice of bread for sandwiches.
Variation: For tuna salad, serve a portion of the combined ingredients on a bed of lettuce with crackers.

❦ 464 ❦

Tuna Melt Open Face Sandwiches
Follow recipe above for Tuna Salad and spread on bread. Top each slice of tuna on bread with a slice of your favorite cheese. We like extra-sharp cheddar. Place on a baking tray under the broiler until the cheese melts and the tuna is warmed. Serve immediately while hot.

❦ 465 ❦

Cooked Play Dough (for playing—not eating!)
Here's a play dough that won't harm little ones if they happen to eat some.
Mix together:
1 c. flour
½ c. salt
2 t. cream of tartar
Add:
1 T. cooking oil
1 c. water
Drops of food coloring
Cook in a non-stick pan or an electric skillet over medium heat. Stir constantly as the mixture thickens

quickly. Cook until the dough forms a ball. This takes approximately three minutes. Knead on wax paper until smooth and cool. Store in an airtight container to keep from drying out. Refrigerate for a longer shelf life.

Note: Use cookie cutters to form fun shapes and figures with the dough.

🜲 *466* 🜲

Cool Carrots

2 lb. carrots, chopped into coins
1 can tomato soup
½ c. salad oil
1 c. sugar
¾ c. vinegar
1 t. dry mustard
1 c. bell pepper, chopped
1 medium sweet onion, chopped

Boil carrots in a pot of water until tender and drain in a colander. Then place drained carrots in a large bowl. Add the soup, oil, sugar, vinegar and dry mustard to a pot and stir. Simmer on low heat for 5 minutes. Pour over carrots and marinate for 24 hours minimum. Will keep for weeks in the refrigerator.

﷽ *467* ﷽

Carob Cow Patties
Yield: 1½ dozen
2 c. carob chips
3 T. shortening
½ c. dry roasted salted peanuts
½ c. raisins
¼ to ⅓ c. coconut flakes (optional)
Fill the bottom of a double boiler ⅓ with water and warm on the stove. In the top pot of the double boiler, melt the carob chips and shortening. Stir off and on until melted and smooth. Turn off the heat and add the remaining ingredients in with the carob. Drop by tablespoons on a tray covered with wax paper. Set the tray in the freezer until the cow patties harden. Remove from tray and store in the refrigerator.

❧ *468* ❧

Ham-and-Cheese Macaroni Casserole
Makes great use of leftover ham. Even those that aren't particularly fond of macaroni and cheese like this dish. Serves 4 to 6.
3 c. cooked macaroni, drained in colander
Dice and sauté 1 small onion in half-stick of butter with 1 small bell pepper
Add to casserole dish:
30 oz. diced tomatoes
macaroni
2½ to 3 c. chopped cooked ham
Sautéed onion and bell pepper
1 c. grated extra-sharp cheddar
1 c. mayonnaise
Stir to coat. Sprinkle ½ c. grated cheese on top (optional). Bake at 350°F for 40 minutes, uncovered. Remove casserole dish with pot holders from oven and serve hot.

Cooking Utensils and their Uses

There are many gadgets used in the kitchen. Whether you plan to bake brownies, fry chicken, or toss a green salad, there are utensils that will be necessary to help you accomplish that task. Here is a list of basic kitchen utensils. With the help of an experienced cook, identify each of these items in your own kitchen and learn its appropriate name and purpose. Then, set them on a table and see how many you can name by yourself.

Utensils for Measuring

Dry and liquid measuring cups—various fractions of a cup and cup, pint, and quart measures
Measuring spoons—set of standard
Metal spatula—for leveling dry measurements
Large spoon or small scoop—for filling measuring cups

Utensils for Mixing

Pastry blender or blending fork—for cutting in shortening (you can also use two table knives)
Long-handled wooden spoons—for stirring sauces, icings, etc.
Rotary eggbeater—for blending icings, etc.
Wire whip—beats air into egg whites
Rubber spatula—removing icing from bowls, folding batter, etc.
Mixing bowls—various sizes

Utensils for Chopping, Grating, Peeling, Slicing, and Other Basic Food Preparations

Vegetable brush—for scrubbing vegetables clean under running water

Colander—for rinsing berries, tomatoes, etc. under running water and for draining pastas, etc.

Vegetable grater—to grate or shred cheese, chocolate, fruit, or vegetables

Vegetable peeler—to remove skins of vegetables

Cutting board—for chopping

Paring knife—for slicing and dicing

Slicing knife—for carving

Serrated bread knife—slicing bread and whole tomatoes

Butcher knife 6" or 8"—cuts raw meat

Sieve—for straining

Utensils, Pots, and Pans for Range Top Cooking

Skillet—frying or sautéing
Saucepan and lid
Stockpot—cook large quantities of sauces, etc.
Pancake turner
Slotted spoons—to drain off liquid or oil
Soup ladle
Spatula
2 pot holders
Double boiler—melting chocolate, butter, etc.
Wok—for stir fry
Teakettle
Tongs—for turning meat without piercing the skin

Utensils for Baking, Roasting, Broiling

Baking sheets, without sides and with low sides
Cooking turner—removing hot cookies or biscuits from baking tray
Pastry brush—oiling cake, muffin, bread pans and baking sheets
Rolling pin—rolling out pie shells, biscuits, jelly rolls, etc.
Bread or pastry board—rolling out pie shells, biscuits, jelly rolls, cookies, kneading bread, etc.

Pie pans
Sifter
Loaf pans—for baking breads and meatloaves
Casserole pans, various quart sizes
Cake pans
Muffin pan—quick breads and meatloaves
Dutch oven with lid—for stew, etc.
Oven mitts
Meat fork
Carving knife

Miscellaneous Kitchen Utensils and Supplies

Apple corer-peeler
Aprons
Can opener, bottle opener, jar opener
Cutters, various sizes and shapes for cookies, biscuits,
pancakes, doughnuts
Food mill—for grinding
Funnels—for filling jars and bottles
Molds—for Jell-O, rice rings, punch bowl rings
Potato masher
Strainers
Timer
Towels, dishcloths

Glossary of Cooking Terms

Bake   To cook in the oven

Baste   To brush or pour liquid over food dring the cooking process

Beat   To mix ingredients fast with a fork, spoon, or beater until smooth

Blend   To mix several ingredients thoroughly, often accomplished in a blender

Boil   To cook liquid until it is so hot that it comes to the boiling stage

Broil   To cook directly under heat. Most ovens are equipped with a broiler

Charbroil   To cook directly over coals on a grill

Chill   To refrigerate or ice to lower the temperature of the food

Chop   To cut in small pieces with a knife on a cutting board

Combine   To mix the ingredients

Cream   To beat until smooth and fluffy

Cube To cut food into square pieces (6 equal sides) generally larger than ¼ inch (see **dice** below)

Cut in To mix butter or shortening in with dry ingredients, using two knives, a pastry blender, or grater

Dice To cut food into small square uniform cubes (see **cube** above)

Dot To add small pieces (pats) of one food (such as butter) onto another

Drizzle To pour a thin strand of liquid (such as honey or syrup) across the top of another food substance or beverage

Dust To sprinkle with a dry ingredient (such as flour or sugar)

Flake To break apart when forked (baked fish flakes easily when done)

Flour To coat exterior of a food product with flour (An easy way to coat chicken pieces or potatoes with flour is to first place flour in a paper sack, add the food, twist the top of the bag, hold it closed, and shake)

Fold To gently combine ingredients with a rubber spatula or spoon

Fry, Deep Fry To cook in hot cooking oil or fat. When deep frying, the food product is usually in a metal fry basket and submerged into the hot cooking oil or fat

Garnish   Adding a decorative finishing touch (such as parsley or lemon) to a plate in order to make the food look attractive

Grate   To rub food up and down against a grater until it is cut into thin shreds

Grease   To brush, rub, or spray a thin coating of oil or fat on the surface of a baking tray or pan to prevent the food from sticking

Grind   To convert food into tiny particles by crushing in a food grinder or grain mill (Wheat, for example, is ground into flour)

Knead   A process used in breadmaking of folding and pressing down dough using the heels of the hand.

Ladle   To dip and serve a liquid with a long handle dipper (used to serve soups and punch)

Marinate   The process of pouring a vinegar-based mixture over foods and allowing it to sit for a period of hours until the flavors have blended or the meat has tenderized

Melt   to heat a food product (such as butter or chocolate) to the point of becoming a liquid

Mince   To finely chop food into tiny pieces (onions are often minced)

Mix   To combine ingredients together with a stirring motion

Pare   To cut off the outer skin of a vegetable or fruit with a knife

Peel   To remove the outer skin off vegetables or fruits by stripping off with a vegetable peeler

Pit   To remove the center seed in a fruit or vegetable

Preheat   To warm the oven or pan to a specific temperature before adding the food

Sauté   To cook food in a pan on top of the stove in butter until tender (Mushrooms are often sautéed)

Scald   To heat milk almost to the point of boiling. Bubbles will appear around the edges when it is hot (Overheating may cause the milk to burn)

Shred   To cut into thin, long strips

Sift   To put dry ingredients through a sifter or sieve (Flour is generally sifted)

Simmer   To cook foods containing liquid slowly in a pot over low heat

Slice   To cut into slices for serving (Roasts and hams are sliced)

Steam   To cook foods in the steam that arises from a lower pan of boiling water

Stir   To mix in a circular motion using a spoon to thoroughly combine ingredients

Toss To mix lightly (Salad greens are tossed to combine and dressings are tossed into slaws)

Whip To rapidly beat using an electric mixer or rotary eggbeater (Egg whites are whipped until light and fluffy)

Dining Etiquette

Setting the Table

Setting the table properly and attractively will ensure that the delicious meal you prepared will look appetizing and appealing to others. Taking the time to set the table nicely shows others that you are hospitable, considerate, and thoughtful. The table doesn't have to look nice just when company is expected. Our family members are special, too. The table should be set handsomely as often as possible. Here are the basic rules for setting the table for a regular sitdown family meal.

1. Position each plate and flatware one inch up from the edge of the table.
2. The fork goes to the left of the plate and the knife and spoons to the right. The knife goes closest to the plate with the blade facing the plate. The spoon is positioned to the right of the knife. The napkin is folded and placed next to the fork. If a salad fork or soup spoon is required, the silverware should be placed down in order of use, working from the

outside in. For example, the salad fork would go on the outside, then the dinner fork.

3. Drinking glasses should be placed directly above the tip of the knife. If coffee or hot tea will be served, cups and saucers should be located to the right of the spoon at each place setting.

4. If a salad plate is used, it should be positioned to the left of the forks if it will be eaten as part of the main course. The napkin can then be set in the dinner plate instead of next to the fork for convenience.

5. If the salad is to be eaten alone as the first course, the salad plate or bowl should be placed in the dinner plate.

6. When bread and butter plates are desired at each place setting, position them directly above the forks.
7. When an arrangement of flowers is used as a centerpiece, it should be low enough so as not to block the view of those seated at the table.
8. The room should be quiet and free from excess noise that will interfere with conversation during meals. Do not leave the television, videos, or radio on during mealtime.

Good Table Manners

Demonstrating good manners at the dinner table is a fine way to show gratitude to the cook for his or her efforts. When the cook uses good manners when serving the meal, it shows warmth and hospitality and makes everyone at the table feel welcome and cared for. Good manners make the whole meal enjoyable for everyone. Follow these rules for good table manners:

1. See that all guests are seated before seating yourself.
2. Wait until the host or hostess begins to eat before eating.
3. Place your napkin in your lap at the beginning of the meal.

4. Arms and elbows are to be kept off the table. When you aren't using your left hand, it should rest in your lap.

5. Chew your food slowly. Don't eat as if you are starving, even if you feel very hungry. Eat slowly, chew your food well. Digestion begins as you chew your food. Chew with your mouth shut. Don't imitate a cement mixer!

6. Never talk with food in your mouth.

7. Meal time isn't just about eating. Look up from your plate while chewing. Make eye contact with the person that is speaking. Be a good listener and take an interest in what others discuss. Don't dominate the conversation.

8. If a very hot serving dish is in front of you, offer to serve others' plates.

9. Pass a dish after you have served yourself without waiting for others to ask. Pass food carefully, using both hands. Always pass to a person's left, so they can serve themselves with their right hand while holding the dish with their left.

10. Use your napkin to gently pat your mouth during the meal or if you must cough.

11. To eat a roll properly, tear it into pieces and butter each piece individually just before eating it. Cut

food into small bites as you eat. Never hurriedly cut everything on your plate.

12. Meals aren't meant to be rushed. Mealtime should be relaxing. Enjoy those around you. Make conversation when there is a moment or two of silence. Discuss pleasant things. Never criticize others, debate, or argue at the table. Do not accept phone calls during evening meals unless its an emergency. If you must answer the phone, excuse yourself and take the call in another room. Return to the dinner table as quickly as possible.

13. Beverage glasses should be refilled from the person's right side.

14. When you have finished eating, place the silverware at the ten o'clock and two o'clock position across the top of your plate.

15. Stay seated at the table until everyone else has finished eating. Always compliment the cook on the meal and show your gratitude.

16. After dinner, read a poem or essay or an inspiring passage of scripture to others when time and the situation permit.

17. Offer to help with the dishes. Dishes should be collected from the person's right side.

Resources

Besides all the tips, recipes, and ideas we've included within this book, a list follows of my own personal kitchen and cooking resources. Not all the books I've listed are current. Some of the most helpful books I have come across in furthering my kitchen skills and knowledge have been the out-of-print ones. But with the popularity of used-book stores, Web sites, and cookbook collectors, I thought it would be fun to share with you my personal kitchen library favorites. Find a shelf or two to start your own kitchen library if you haven't already done so. Keep a look out for the older books noted here when perusing used book and thrift stores, antiques and junk shops, yard and estate sales, auctions and flea markets.

Books

Adams, Jean Prescott. *Meatless Meals*. Albert Whitman & Co., 1936.
Complete with meatless menu ideas for those of us brought up to plan meals around meat. Learn how to make your own frostings and fillings, appetizers, salad dressings, sauces, soups, and nut and vegetable loaves.

American Rabbit Breeder's Association. *Domestic Rabbit Cook Book*. Bloomington, IL.
Tried-and-true recipes. Don't have rabbit meat? Don't dismay, most rabbit recipes can be prepared using poultry with equally satisfying results.

Arkin, Frieda. *The Essential Kitchen Gardener: An A to Z Guide to Growing What You Eat*. Galahad Books, 1996.
A must read for the kitchen garden cook. Highly valuable information for both cooks and gardeners.

Bond, Jill. *Dinner's in the Freezer!* GCB Publishing, 1993.
An efficient cook is organized and plans ahead. This book helps you get started on that track.

Carroll, Ricki and Robert Carroll. *Cheesemaking Made Easy*. Garden Way Publishing, 1995.
This book covers the basics of cheesemaking including equipment needed, directions for making soft cheeses: cream and cottage; hard cheeses: cheddar and Gouda; whey cheeses: ricotta; and goat's milk cheeses: feta. There are 60 cheesemaking recipes in all. A must-have guide for the owner of a dairy goat, sheep, or cow as well as anyone who enjoys cooking with delicious cheeses. It is so gratifying to make it

yourself. This book takes the intimidation away from cheesemaking.

Chesman, Andrea. *Pickles and Relishes.* Garden Way Publishing, Storey Communications, 1991.
Calling all pickle-loving connoisseurs. Pickles beyond the cucumber from apples to zucchini, learn how with 150 interesting recipes.

Cooper, Jane. *Woodstove Cookery.* Storey Books, 1977.
Want the warmth, charm, and versatility of cooking and heating on a wood cookstove? Got caught last winter without a source for cooking? Learn how to shop for a stove, install it, maintain it, and cook on it. Recipes included. There is a knack to cooking on a woodstove. If you were raised on gas and electric stoves, you'll need this book to help you learn the techniques and tips for woodstove cooking.

Cottrell, Edyth Young. *The Oats, Peas, Beans & Barley Cookbook.* Woodbridge Press, Second Edition, Tenth Printing, 1983.
Written by a professional nutritionist, this book features 450 recipes of natural, unprocessed foods, no-animal based cooking. This book helps retrain the traditional cook to be more nutritionally minded in her cooking.

Eliason, Karine and Nevada Harward and Madeline Westover. *Make-A-Mix,* Fisher Books, 1995.
A book that has sold over 1,000,000 copies. The smart way to cook. Making your own mixes guarantees the quality of the food you serve your family and guests. They make great gifts, too.

Ely, Leanne, C.N.C. *Healthy Foods,* Champion Press, 2001.
Includes over 100 family-approved recipes for cooking healthy and tasty meals.

Fuller, Lucy. *Whole Foods for Whole People.* Teach Services, Inc., 1994.
Serious about good nutrition and healthy eating and lifestyle? This book is a must. Strictly vegetarian based, it excludes egg and milk products as well. Book endorsed by Agatha Thrash, M.D.

Betty Crocker's Picture Cook Book, General Mills, First Edition, 1950. 50th Anniversary edition, 2000.
This is the book I used as a beginning cook. It covers the basics thoroughly for the new cook and helps one to master the art of bread baking and elegant dessert dishes for the advanced. In honor of its fiftieth anniversary, a special commemorative edition was published in 2000. If I had to choose or recommend only one cookbook to own, this would be it!

Handslip, Carole. *Vegetarian Cooking,* Octopus Books Limited, 1980.
From pies, omelets, quiche, salads and flapjacks—a variety of recipes featuring fresh vegetables, cheeses, eggs, nuts, and grains.

Hobson, Phyllis. *Making & Using Dried Foods,* Garden Way Publishing, 1995.
Dehydrating foods saves on storage space. This book covers the basics of drying fruits, vegetables, herbs, meats, dairy products, and grains, and how to make soup mixes, selecting a dehydrator, and even plans for building one. Complete guide to dehydrating with recipes included for cooking with your dried-food products.

Lacalamita, Tom. *The Ultimate Bread Machine Cookbook.* Simon & Schuster, 1993.
I was surprised at how much I learned about bread making from this book. I never though that a bread machine or a bread machine cookbook could be a key to furthering my bread-making skills. But with this book, the door to better bread building has been opened. Besides making tasty loaves of bread in a modern bread machine, this book teaches you how to take the dough and hand fashion bread sticks, calzones, braids, bagels, doughnuts, and danishes. I can attest to the luscious

flavor of many of these delightful recipes. What a sense of accomplishment after making such delectable dainties as danishes. Over 100 recipes included. Love bread? You'll love this cookbook!

Leisure Arts, Inc. *Gifts of Good Taste.* Memories in the Making Series, Leisure Arts, Inc., 1989.
Beautifully combines the arts of cooking and crafting. Recipes for making mixes, relishes, jellies, mints, and more, then demonstrates a lovely way of presenting them as gifts or for sale. Beautiful color photographs of each food product presented.

Livingston, A.D. *Cast-Iron Cooking.* Lyons Press, 1991.
A must read for the wood-stove owner as well as the country cook. Cast-iron cooking is an American classic tradition. Learn how with these great recipes.

MacRae, Norma M., R.D. *Canning and Preserving Without Sugar.* Globe Pequot, 1993.
At last, instructions for making jams, jellies, and canning fruits without sugar. Learn how to can and cook with fruit juices and honey instead. A healthier approach to jelly making—hooray!

McCoy, Jonni. *Miserly Moms.* Full Quart Press, 1996.
Besides all the frugal tips for saving money for those desiring to be stay-at-home moms, this book has

some wonderful recipes for making your own salad dressings, sauces, pancakes, and more to save you money.

Seranne, Ann. *The Complete Book of Home Preserving.* Doubleday & Company, 1955.
Complete indeed! A comprehensive guide to home preserving from fish to fruit.

Sturges, Lena E. *Our Best Recipes.* Southern Living, 1970.
1,500 recipes from beverages to vegetables. From the best cooks in the south, the readers of *Southern Living* magazine. A must-have for those on both sides of the Mason-Dixon line.

Vegetarian Cooking—Exciting Ideas for Delicious Meals. Sweetwater Press, 1996. Recipes to enhance vegetable and grain preparations. Beautifully photographed.

Taylor-Hough, Deborah. *Frozen Assets Lite & Easy.* Champion Press, Ltd, 2001.
The only efficient way to freeze meals ahead. Starts with the main ingredients and gives recipes for making many low-fat entrees with them. Poultry, pork, beef, tuna, and even some vegetarian meals featuring eggplant are included.

Tukua, Deborah S., *Pearls of Country Wisdom: Hints From a Small Town on Keeping Garden and Home,* Lyons Press, 2000.
Encompassing every aspect of country living for the cook interested in making it herself. Learn how to conjure up honey-butter, liquid soap, kitchen cleaners, breakfast cereals, yogurt, herbal teas, home remedies, home can chili, and firestarters. Kitchen tips for efficiency, flavoring, and food storage all are included. Over 700 tips, recipes, and great ideas.

Tukua, Deborah S., and West, Vicki. *Pearls of Garden Wisdom,* Lyons Press, 2001.
After reading all the helpful tips for raising wonderful fruits, vegetables, and even edible flowers, try some of their family favorite recipes for enjoying the fruits of the vine, tree, and plant.

Wilson, Mimi and Lagerborg, Mary Beth. *Once-A-Month Cooking,* Focus on the Family, 1986. The pair that made once-a-month cooking popular today. Learn from the queens of home-made freezer meals.

Magazines

These are magazines that you probably won't find on the shelves of your major retail outlets, but are well worth reading.

Coming Home Magazine
P.O. Box 187, Canmer, KY 42722
Web site: www.cominghomemag.bookpub.net
Email: cominghome@mail.com
A journal of practical Christian living. Published bimonthly; $20 annual subscription
Topics include: housekeeping, cooking, canning, recipes, home birth, homeschooling, parenting, devotionals, home remedies, gardening, and how-to projects for country living.
Articles by Deborah S. Tukua appear in each issue.

An Encouraging Word
P.O. Box 374, Covert, MI 49043
For women of all ages. Published quarterly; $22 annual subscription
Topics include: home birth, homemaking, homecooking, homesteading, home business, homeschooling, hospitality, and the inspirational.

Keepers at Home
2727 Township Road 421, Sugarcreek, OH 44681
In the Spirit of Titus Two. Published quarterly; $9 annual subscription
Topics include: cooking, canning, homemaking, herbs, kitchen gardens, and devotionals.

Countryside Magazine
P.O. Box 6017, Duluth, MN 55806-6017
Web site: http://www.countrysidemag.com
(800) 551-5691
The magazine of modern homesteading. Published bi-monthly; $18 annual subscription
Topics include: country cooking, recipes, gardening, herbs, livestock, building your own home, and how-to projects for every aspect of rural living. A wealth of country know-how.

Web Sites

Bornagn Farms—www.bornagn.com
John and Lori Banks
4266 Old Rome Pike
Lenanon, TN 37087
(877) EAT-WEET Email: info@Bornagn.com

Features premium whole grains, baking equipment and supplies, dehydrated foods, books of health, nutrition and country living.

Health For You—Sandi Krawkoski
www.healthforyouministry.com
Email: info@healthforyouministry.com
P.O. Box 180327
Utica, MI 48318-0327
Putting health back into your baking. Site includes free baking recipes to print out. Offers grain mills, bread mixers, pressure canners/cookers, dehydrators, juicers, cookbooks, and other kitchen equipment as well.

Homespun Ideas—Pasqualucci family
http://homespun-ideas.com
Includes country-cooking recipes that you can print out as well as gardening and other homesteading information. They also publish a free weekly Email newsletter. Subscribe by Email to:
webmastermail@homespun-ideas.com.

Miserly Moms—Jonni McCoy
www.miserlymoms.com
Focus on frugal living and cooking on a fixed budget. Multitudes of recipes shared by readers.

My Front Porch—Trish Good
http://freeweb.pdq.net/shanearthur/index.html
Email requests to: porch@pdq.net

The 21st Century Homekeeper—Sylvia Britton
www.geocites.com/Heartland/Hills/9684/home.html
Tips for kitchen, cooking and home as well as wonderful recipes, some passed down for generations. A warm and charming site.

Catalogs

The Beautiful Girlhood Collection
The Vision Forum, Inc.
32335 U.S. Hwy., 281 North
Bulverde, TX 78163-3158
(800) 440-0022
www.visionforum.com
Beautiful color catalog featuring a fine porcelain floral tea service, vintage kitchen apron, wooden spoon set, hardwood rolling pin, and mixing bowls for mother's little helpers in the kitchen. A lovely way to welcome your daughters to the world of cooking and Victorian tea parties.

Country Store
5925 Country Lane, P.O. Box 990
Greendale, WI 53129-0990
(800) 558-1013
Cute country charm. Helpful kitchen gadgets, country cookbooks, apple dishes, and accessories await you. (This is a division of Reiman Publications, LLC.)

Domestications
Kitchen & Garden
P.O. Box 66
Hanover, PA 17333-0066
(800) 245-3399
Charming, trendy kitchen furnishings, stainless cookware, kitchen organizer items, and appliances.

Falls Mill and Country Store, Est. 1873
John and Jane Lovett, owners
134 Falls Mill Road
Belvidere, TN 37306
(931) 469-7161
A National Registry historic site, built in 1873 and operated by a 32-foot overshot water-powered grain mill. Home of the Museum of Power and Industry, Inc. A lovely, quaint place to tour in a beautiful setting in south-central Tennessee with its waterwheel, situated

on a tranquil creekside. Offers fresh stone-ground flour and meal products: yellow and white cornmeal, pancake mix, and flour. All charmingly packaged and affordable. Makes great gifts.

King Arthur Flour Baker's Catalogue
Sands, Taylor & Wood Company
Box 1010
Norwich, VT 05055
(800) 827-6836
The ultimate in baking ingredients for those who don't grind their own wheat into flour.

Lehman's
Box 41
One Lehman Circle
Kidron, OH 44636
(330) 857-1330
Purveyors of nonelectric household items. They've been serving the Amish community in Ohio for generations. Great source for cast-iron cookware, canning supplies, and general kitchen equipment. Also carry many good cookbooks and country-living books.

Williams-Sonoma
Mail Order Department
P.O. Box 7456
San Francisco, CA 04120-7456
(800) 541-1262 Customer Service
(800) 541-2233 Orders
High-quality kitchen equipment, cookware and supplies, beautiful dishes, tableware, holiday foods and fine kitchen furnishings, lovely color catalog.

Index

Free Dog Food (recipe), 165
freezer, power outage and, 142
French Dressing (recipe), 215
French toast, 103, 130, 156, 213
Fresh Apple Cake (recipe), 223
Fresh Broccoli and Bacon Salad (recipe),
  235
Fried Dandelion Blossoms (recipe), 236
fried foods, 90
Fried Venison Steak (recipe), 246–47
frosted cakes, 71, 76
Frozen Assets Lite & Easy (Taylor-Hough),
  287
Frozen Yogurt (recipe), 192
fruit bowls, 24
fruit flies, 45
fruit juices, 91, 117, 127
fruit salad, 126
fruits, 146, 147, 150
funnels, 267

garlic, 94, 96, 152
garnishes, 99, 100
gas fish cookers, 142, 148
gas stoves, 143
gelatin powder, 73
gift baskets/boxes, 130–31, 149, *149*
Gifts of Good Taste (Leisure Arts, Inc.),
  286
ginger, 96
gingerbread cookies, 77, *77*
gingham, 21
glass containers. *See* jars
glassware, 17, 26, 37
glossary, 269–73
goat meat, 165
goat's milk, 91, 114
Good and Easy Pizza (recipe), 241
grain mills, 95
Grannie's Buttermilk Biscuits (recipe),
  199
granola, making, 189
grape jelly, 150
Grape Juice (recipe), 171
graters, 45, 46, 53–54, 265
gravy, 92, 106
grease, 35, 36, 123
grease fires, 60
Great Northern Beans (recipe), 162–63

green beans, drying, 7
griddles, greasing, 129–30
grilled foods, 90
groceries, 32
grocery lists, 54
Growing Green Salad Sprouts (recipe),
  224–25

Ham-and-Cheese Macaroni Casserole
  (recipe), 261
hands
  "dishpan," 34
  washing, 48
hangers, 41
hard-shell clams, 105
Health for You (Web site), 291
Healthy Foods (Ely), 284
herbal teas, 91, 130
herbs, 2, 20, 94, 99, 151
Home-Style Cream of ____ Soup
  (recipe), 230–31
Homemade Butter (recipe), 183–85
Homemade Granola (recipe), 189
Homemade Honey Graham Crackers
  (recipe), 202–3
Homemade Pear or Apple Sauce
  (recipe), 221–22
Homemade Soup Stock (recipe), 230
Homespun Ideas (Web site), 291
honey, 45, 82, 90, 92, 108
Honey Barbecue Sauce (recipe), 217
Honey-Butter (recipe), 185
Honey Mustard Dressing, 234
Honey Mustard Slaw (recipe), 167
Honey-Strawberry Syrup (recipe), 208
hot dishes, 40
Hot Lemon-Mint Tea (recipe), 196
hot pads, 5
hot peppers, 96
Hot Spiced Apple Cider (or Tea)
  (recipe), 194
Hush Puppies (recipe), 200–201

ice chests, 33
ice cream, 33
ice-cream buckets, 42, 55
ice-cream-cone drips, 117
ice-cream scoops, 46
ice cube trays, 99, 109

timers, 267
tin cans, 5
toast, 124
Tomato and Lima Bean Salad (recipe),
    226–27
tomatoes, 104–5, 108
    green, 111, 227
    knives for, 116
tongs, 129, 266
toothbrushes, 46
towels, 21, 267
Trail Mix Snack (recipe), 190
Treasure Chip Cookies (recipe), 218
trellises, 16
trivets, 19
tuna, 91
Tuna Melt Open Face Sandwiches
    (recipe), 258
Tuna Salad Sandwiches (recipe), 257
turkey, deboning, 103
turnips, 110
21st Century Homekeeper, The (Web
    site), 292

Ultimate Bread Machine, The (Lacalamita),
    285–86
utensils, 53–54, 263–67

vases, 5
vegetable brushes, 265
Vegetable Stew (recipe), 158–59
vegetables, 91, 109
    canning, 146, 147
    cooking, 122
    grating, 59
    liquids from, 127
    nutrients in, 121
    preventing spoilage of, 140
Vegetarian Cooking (Handslip), 285
*Vegetarian Cooking—Exciting Ideas for
    Delicious Meals,* 287
venison, 165, 246–47
vests, 18, *18*
vinegar, 42, 91, 94, 116
    cider, 136, 141, 150
    flavored, 150, 151
    frying doughnuts and, 123
    herbed, 130
    recipe for, 153

white distilled, 151
    wine, 152
Vinegar from Cider (recipe), 193
vines, growing, 16
violets, 100
vitamin C, 68–69, 110, 147
vitamins, 2, 20
votive candles, 17

waffles, 130, 156
wagon wheels, 12
Waldorf Salad (recipe), 256–57
wall decorations, 24
wallpaper, 10, 52
walnuts, 134
washbasins, 22, 23, 24
washing hands, 48
water-bath canning, 144, 167–71
watercress, 92
watermelons, 136, 195
Web sites, 290–92
wheat berries, 96
wheat grass, 155, 197
Wheat Grass–Apple Juice Slush Drink
    (recipe), 197
whipped cream, 182
white refined sugar, 90, 91–92
white rice, 90
white wine, 151
Whole Foods for Whole People (Fuller),
    284
whole-grain pastas, 90
Williams-Sonoma (catalog), 295
window valances, 5, 7, 8
wine, 150–51
wine racks, 4
wire baskets, 4
wire whips, 264
wooden spoons, 264
Woodstove Cookery (Cooper), 283

yeast, 68
yogurt, 91, 94
    frozen, 192
    making, 114, 187–88
Yogurt Cream Cheese (recipe),
    192
yogurt cups, 55–56